Educational Psychology

An Interactive Classroom Approach

Published by:
Lotus Press

Educational Psychology

(An Interactive Classroom Approach)

Stella Reynolds

Lotus PRESS

4735/22, Prakash Deep Building
Ansari Road, Darya Ganj,
New Delhi-110002

Lotus Press : Publishers & Distributors
Unit No. 220, 2nd Floor, 4735/22, Prakash Deep Building,
Ansari Road, Darya Ganj, New Delhi- 110002
Ph.: 32903912, 23280047 • E-mail : lotus_press@sify.com
www.lotuspress.co.in

EDUCATIONAL PSYCHOLOGY
(An Interactive Classroom Approach)

ISBN: 81-8382-072-7
Reprint : 2011

Published by **Lotus Press,** New Delhi-110002
Printed at : Concept Imprint, Delhi

PREFACE

Educational Psychology is written with the purpose of developing a meaningful understanding of the role of educational psychology in classroom teaching. It provides clear connections between theories of learning and motivation and a variety of important interactive approaches to classrooms.

To help readers become intentional teachers, this book offers a set of questions to guide them and models best practices through classroom examples. It prepares teachers as no other text does. It teaches them to think about how students develop and learn, to make decisions before and during instruction, and to consider what constitutes evidence that their students are learning and succeeding. An interactive classroom approach is conceived and designed with the idea that learning is the core focus of educational psychology and that it can be fostered through active engagement with theory and applications.

Editor

CONTENTS

CONTENTS

1

INTRODUCTION

Educational psychology is the modern science, which applies the findings of psychology to the learning and development of human beings. The knowledge of educational psychology helps the teachers to understand the inner potentialities, which underlie the behaviour of the learner. So generally educational psychology as applied branch of psychology deals with the teaching learning process, guidance and counselling.

Learning is considered as outcomes of teaching process teacher is equipped as model role through educational psychology. This branch provides knowledge about all aspects related to teaching learning process. As well it provides the knowledge about different theories of psychologists, which bear the ample role in educational setting. More this branch of psychology bears the knowledge and understanding of disturbed students and conflict resolution then it enables the teacher to teach and treat them according to their differences.

The main purpose of all these efforts is to make the teaching learning process effective and to acquaint the teacher about mastery learning. Keeping in view the focus of educational psychology comprises on "quality education" teacher may work as counsellor and guide and can provide the concerned counselling and guidance services, which are needed to students. Broadly educational psychology focuses the following areas:

a) Learner

b) Learning

c) Teaching

d) Guidance and Counselling

Educational psychology consists of two words psychology and other is education. Former deals with scientific study of individual and later aims at the all round and balanced development of a person. How can this purpose be achieved or how may education system be made "student centered". This is only possible if the educative process would be organised on the basis of study of the student's personality. For this purpose merely educational psychology helps. Because it deals with the study of student, for knowing his natural requirements, attitudes, aptitudes, abilities and potentials etc., on the other side this branch will help to explore the skills, techniques, methods and approaches for making the teaching—learning process effective.

Where the educational psychology makes the teaching learning process qualitative. There it is helpful for providing the counselling to the students. Many students face the different problems related to their study relationships with their teachers and fellows, emotional and social adjustment etc., a teacher may feel difficulty for counseling to his/her students. In this critical situation only educational psychology supports the teacher in providing the guidance and counselling for solving the problems of students.

Precisely educational psychology is functioning duly, it makes teaching-learning process effective and provides the counseling to the students. The field of education psychology is concerned with all psychological aspects of educational process, its primary goal is to discover how people learn. Following are the important characteristics of the nature of educational psychology:

— It combines two fields i.e. education and psychology.

— It is the scientific study of human behaviour in educational situations.

— It is one of the many branches of applied psychology. It is concerned with those factors, principles, and techniques which relate to the various aspects of student's development.

— It is concerned with learning situation and the process by which learning can be made more efficient and effective.

— Educational psychology is not as exact as natural sciences, since the human behaviour cannot be predicted exactly.

— Educational psychology is a science of education dealing primarily with how, when and what of education.

IMPORTANCE OF EDUCATIONAL PSYCHOLOGY

Educational psychology is the science of education, which mainly deals with the problems of teaching and helps the teachers in his task of modifying the learner's behaviour and bringing about an all-round development of his personality. For analysing the scope of educational psychology these questions must be answered:

a) Who is being educated?

b) By whom is the learner to be taught?

c) What is to be taught?

d) How are the learning experiences to be provided?

e) When and where are the learning experiences to be provided?

FUNCTIONS OF EDUCATIONAL PSYCHOLOGY

- The knowledge of the nature of the student.
- Understanding of the nature, aims and purposes of education.
- Understanding of the scientific methods and procedures which have been used in arriving at the facts and principles of educational psychology.
- The principles and techniques of learning and teaching.
- Training in methods of measuring abilities and achievement in subjects.
- Knowledge of the growth and development of students.
- The better adjustment of students and to help to prevent maladjustment.
- Knowledge of the educational significance and control of emotions.
- An understanding of the principles and techniques of correct training.

PERSONALITY

A distinct or unique method of approaching or influencing one another. This uniqueness of a person is generally known as personality. It covers the whole nature of the individual. Psychology does not regard personality as a passive entity but as that dynamic character of the individual, which finds expression through his conduct and activities. It does not enquire into what personality is but into what does. Personality is the unity or integration of manifold manifestations like pleasure, love, hate, activity, inactivity and hope, despair of the individual. Nature of personality are:

— Personality is a whole rather than the parts.

— Personality implies an integration of various traits.

— Personality represents a unique integration of traits so as to differentiate one person from another on the basis of this very quality. Personality is the results of both heredity and environment.

— Personality is composed of traits, which are by and large learned or acquired.

— Each personality can be identified with some motive forces.

Personality Development

Our personality is formed through various developmental stages. The forces operating on it are both genetic and environmental. Three types of personality theory can be specially mentioned for explaining the nature of personality development. These are psychoanalytic, learning and role theories.

Psychoanalytic theory

According to this theory, there is continuity in growth, which begins, in the earliest childhood. The classical psychoanalyst under the leadership of Freud postulated the five stages of development along with its characteristics features as given below:

1. *Oral Stage*: This corresponds to the first year of one's life. The pleasure during this stage is derived through lips, and mouth sucking, eating, and thumb sucking. This is the dependency upon other stage.
2. *Anal Stage*: It begins in the second year of one's life. During this period, pleasure is derived through retention and expulsion of faces and also through muscular control.

3. *Phallic Stage*: This stage begins from the third year and continues through the fifth year of one's life. In this stage pleasure is derived through genital stimulation and associated fantasies. At this stage child's super age (conscience) is formed through identification with parents.
4. *Latency*: It is a dormant period usually beginning from the sixth year until puberty, i.e. roughly the eleventh or twelfth year of one's life. The pleasure is derived from external world, curiosity, knowledge, etc. as substitute gratifications. It corresponds with elementary school age and is important for social development of the child.
5. *Genital stage*: It is the period beginning from adolescence and goes up to adulthood. Here, the pleasure is derived from mature sexual relations with a partner of opposite sex. A person starts his/her practical life.

Learning theories

a) According to the learning theories, the development of personality is dependent to a large degree on the rewards and punishments administered by significant people.

b) Most of the habits, discriminations, generalisations, attitudes and values are acquired this way.

c) The formation of new connections between stimuli and responses acquisition of sign-gestalts and development of insight understandings and critical thinking constitute the foundations of behaviour and through that of personality.

Role theories

— Role theories describe the development of

personality in terms of the manner in which the individual meets the various demands that society makes upon him in this role of child, parent, man woman, worker, citizen.

— It is assumed that the biological individual is adoptable enough to fit a variety of roles; he evidently has to acquire his/her role behaviour through experience with his/her particular culture.

— The main crux of this theory is that the infant is born into certain prearranged role (family, sex, nationality)

— Role behaviour is dependent upon the role positions that society establishes. There are at least five kinds of positions in the societies.

a) Age-sex positions.

b) Occupational positions.

c) Prestige positions (e.g. chief, slave).

d) Family class or household positions.

e) Positions association groups based on congeniality or common interests.

— Occupants of a given position are expected to fulfill the role by behaving in certain way, some kinds of behaviour are prescribed, some are permitted, and some are forbidden. Our personality thus develops in such a way that the relevant role positions may be effectively occupied. In a simple and straight way it may be said that personality development implies the development of the traits of the individual. An individual's personality is determined and built in the present, on the past and for the future. Following traits are helpful for observing the personality of someone for making the decision about; what one is what one was and what one will be?

Factors Affecting the Personality Development

Personal factors

— Physical structure of the individual.
— Emotional reactions.
— Aspirations.
— Aptitudes.
— Attitudes.
— Interests.
— Motivation.
— Intellectual level—thinking, contemplation, reasoning, etc.

Family factors

— Discipline: Protection and Rejection. etc.
— Up bringing of the children.
— No. of children.
— Value placed on the gender of the child.
— Step-parents.
— Nuclear or joint family.
— Accommodation in the house.
— Parents' ambitions and interests.
— Economics, political, religious and social status of the family.

Environmental factors

— Neighborhood, community, peer groups etc.
— Cultural environment.
— Political environment.

— Religious environment.
— Social environment.
— Mass media environment.

Teachers' Role

— A spiritual preceptor as in vedic period.

— A communicator and provider of knowledge.

— A 'learning facilitator'.

— A 'gardener' or 'directress' of learning in the naturalist movement in education.

— A 'manager' of learning activity in the pragmatic philosophy of education.

— An ' ideal person' in the philosophy of idealism.

— A 'soldier' and 'weapon' in nazism and communism.

— An 'agent of social change' in the democratic philosophy.

— A teacher as a 'mediator' between the learner and the subject-matter.

— A teacher as a 'transmitter' of cultural heritage.

— A teacher as the 'educational media user'.

— A teacher as the 'spearhead' of change in the society.

— A teacher as the 'harbinger' of social change.

INDIVIDUAL DIFFERENCES

Socially, all individuals are equal but physically and psychologically all individuals are unequal and in other words each individual is different from the other. Psychological terminology that has been applied to differences between individuals, which makes one as a unique individual is known as individual differences. This term means that different people learn differently. Differences among individuals may be slight, moderate or extreme.

Factors Affecting Individual Differences

a) Heredity factors (Inborn).

b) Environment factors (Learned).

Dimensions of Individual Differences

Broadly speaking there are two dimensions of individual differences

a) Physical differences.

b) Psychological differences.

Physical differences are

— Differences in chronological age.

— Differences in physical maturity.

— Differences in health status.

— Physical fitness and fatigue.

— Differences in appearances.

Psychological differences are

— Emotional differences.

— Intelligence.

— Readiness.

— Curiosity and eagerness to learn.

— Experience of success.

— Attention span.

— Academic performance.

— Differences in abilities, attitudes and traits.

— Differences in achievement.

— Differences in social behaviour.

— Sex differences.

Educational Implications

It is fact that all individuals learn in different way. This difference occurs due to heredity and environment. It is quite clear that the same curriculum, same methods of teaching and same discipline and even the same institution will not serve the individual needs of students. Teachers are well awared that what students' learning may vary from student to student, even when students have been exposed to the same environment. Five broad areas, to be focused:

1. Streaming of grouping of students.
2. Curriculum planning.
3. Disciplinary treatment.
4. Methods of teaching.
5. Guidance and counselling.

Disturbed students

We assume that it is "normal" for students to sit still for extended periods of time and "abnormal" if they cannot. Teachers expect students to behave in certain ways in the classroom: To stay seated for hours at a time, to speak only when called on to conform academically to the norms of their grade, to find the topics of instruction interesting. They regard the student as immature, emotionally disturbed, learning disabled or simply unmanageable.

In all cases teacher's opinions are not correct. Some students from all class may be disturbed who can create problem or they may be got themselves slow in their academic achievements. All disturbed students are essentially maladjusted personalities and this maladjustment is the result of faulty upbringing, improper environmental influences and maltreatment.

Characteristics of disturbance are:

a) Disturbance occurs when goal is blocked.

b) Disturbance lies both in the individual and his/her environment.

c) Disturbance results in mental tension.

d) Disturbance is that stage or condition in which failure dominates the attempt. The intensity of disturbance depends upon the significance of the goal and the strength of the blockade.

Causes of disturbance

The causes may be divided into two heads; Internal and External.

Some internal causes are:

a) Physical abnormality or defects.

b) Conflicting aims and desires.

c) High ideals and morality of the individual.

d) Too high level of aspiration.

e) Lack of persistence.

f) Lack of sincerity.

Some external causes are:

a) Natural calamities.

b) Economic and financial constraints.

c) Corruption and favoritism.

d) Absence of norms and domination of subjectivity.

Reactions of disturbance

Some simple reactions are:

a) Increasing efforts.

b) Improving trials.

c) Adopting compromising positions.

d) Withdrawal from the situation.

e) Submissiveness.

Some violent reactions are:

a) *External aggression*: Quarrelling with colleagues and superiors

b) *Internal aggression*: Hatred for self sometimes may result in suicide

Internal aggression is more dangerous than external aggression.

Managing Disturbed Students

Disturbed students mostly cause the disruptive behaviour in the classroom. Teachers must be aware about it and try to control it. Because ignoring the student's behaviour also sends the message to all students that it is acceptable not to follow the class rules. It would be better for the teacher to explain to the student why the behaviour is inappropriate and indicate the consequences of continuing it. If the behaviour continues, it is important for the teacher to enforce the consequences.

— To meet students basic needs results in much misbehaviour in the classrooms

— To develop an effective teacher-student relationship.

— To focus the students goals or targets.

— To keep the students on—task.

— To create a business like classroom climate in which students understand that they and the teacher have a shared goal: to accomplish activities that promote learning.

— To encourage mutual respect and courtesy.

— To inform all the students about classrooms "rules of conduct" that indicates which behaviours are required and which are prohibited.

— To use punishment but as a last resort.

— To use positive reinforcement effectively.

— To communicate effectively with students.

LEARNING

Learning occupies a very important place in our life. It pervades our life from cradle to grave. Most of what we do or do not do is influenced by what we learn and how we learn it. Learning therefore provides a key to the structure of our personality and behaviour. All the efforts of parents, schools and societies are devoted to the learning of children. Learning is an enrichment of experience. There are three main goals of learning:

a) Acquisition of knowledge.

b) Acquisition of skills.

c) Acquisition of attitudes and ideals.

Theories and Approaches of Learning

What goes into the process of learning? How does an individual learn a set of facts and figures? Skills, habits, interests, attitudes and similar other things in his life? Such questions have always been a subject of enquiry and investigation for psychologists and as a result, a number of theories have come into existence. These theories may be classified under two major heads:

a) Approaches
   — Behaviourist approach.
   — Cognitive approach.
   — Humanistic approach.
   — Social-situational approach.

b) Theories
   — Skinner's Learning Theory.
   — Piaget's Theory.
   — Gagne's Theory.

Skinner learning theory

B.F. skinner, essentially a behaviourist, developed a theory of operant conditioning. According to skinner man is a machine and automation. All the behaviour of man can be described in mechanistic terms. This theory was given in 1931. Skinner called his theory as operant conditioning, as it is based on certain operations or actions, which an organism has to carry out. The basic gist in this theory of conditioning is that an organism tends in the future to do what it was doing at the time of reinforcement.

Operant conditioning explains the learning or shaping of behaviour in terms of response — reinforcement contingency. The new behaviour is said to be acquired by the consequences to an act. These consequences may be either positive (pleasant) or negative (unpleasant) or aversive. Learning is assumed to be the acquisition of new responses through arrangement of reinforcement contingencies. Some of the important operations as mechanism briefly described are as follows:

1. Shaping.
2. Extinction.

3. Spontaneous recovery.
4. Reinforcement.

a. *Shaping*: It refers to the judicious use of selective reinforcement to bring certain desirable changes in behaviour of the organism. The basic process in shaping is successive approximation to the desired behaviour. The experimenter shapes or molds the behaviour of the organism as clay is molded by a potter in a definite form of a pot. Shaping may be used as successful technique for training individuals to learn difficult and complex behaviour and also for introducing desirable modifications in their behaviour.

b. *Chaining*: Where the required behaviour or task is broken down into small steps for its effective learning. But each segment in the chain must be linked to the other.

c. *Discrimination and cueing*: Discrimination is a process of using cues, signals or information to determine when behaviour is likely to be reinforced or punished. The process of discrimination has wide applications in the field of instruction and behaviour modification. For helping the student to learn to discriminate, due care should be taken to provide proper feedback on the correctness or incorrectness of his responses.

d. *Generalisation*: It refers to the ability of an organism dealing with the perception of and response to, similar stimuli. Generalisation may be understood in terms of a learning process where the organism learns to provide similar operant responses, to stimuli similar to but not the same as the training stimulus.

This theory has revolutionised the field of training or learning by putting forward the following practical ideas and implications:

— A behaviour or response is dependent upon its consequences. For training an organism to learn a particular behaviour or response, it may be initiated to respond in such a way as to produce the reinforcing stimulus. The training or learning process and environment must be so designed as to create the minimum frustration and the maximum satisfaction in a learner to provide him with proper reinforcement for the desired training or learning.

— Learning or training objectives should be defined very specifically in terms of behaviours.

— Objectives should be arranged in order of simple to complex.

— For developing motivation in the students for learning, reinforcers like praise, blames, grades etc., should be used.

— Proper use of positive and negative gestures also serves as reinforcers to work.

— Reinforcers should be used periodically so that the possibility of extinction of the desired behaviour is resisted.

— The principle of operant conditioning may be successfully applied in behaviour modification for the principle of immediacy of reinforcement is very important. Praise for a job done well given immediately can be a stronger reinforcer or motivator then a grade given much later.

— This theory does not attribute motivation to internal processes within organism. It provides an external approach to motivation. For example, food is a reinforcer to a rat or a pigeon, and knowledge of the correct response is reinforcement to a learner.

— This theory advocated the avoidance of punishment for unlearning the undesirable behaviour and for shaping the desirable behaviour. Punishment proves ineffective in the long run.

— In it most effective application, the theory of operant conditioning has contributed a lot to the development of teaching machines, programmed learning system and computer-assisted instruction.

Piaget theory

The best-known cognitive-developmental psychologist is 'Jean Piaget'. His work on how people acquire knowledge provoked numerous psychologists to focus on the cognitive processes and to rethink how human learning occurs. The cognitive-development model focuses on changes that occur in how people think as they progress from infancy through childhood and adolescence and ultimately into adulthood.

Piaget viewed children as active learners who behave like "little scientists" who develop their won "theories" about how the world works and set out to confirm these hunches. Piaget's primary concern was to discover how people acquire knowledge, which is often called the "epistemological question". Students constantly create their own knowledge of the world by comparing external evidence with internal understanding.

Infants acquire knowledge based on the sensory experiences of sight, hearing, touch, taste and smell. Preschoolers progress to the stage of acquiring knowledge of the world through their perceptions of their own experiences in the world. Older children begin to apply the rules of logic to understand how the world works. And, finally, adolescents and adults progress to the stage where they can apply logic to hypothetical as well as to real situations. According to Piaget people progress through four sequential stages of cognitive development. Sensori-motor, pre-operations, concrete operations and formal operations. Each stage is characterised by qualitative change in behaviour.

Sensorimotor Stage (From birth to about two years): Infants explore their environments, seeing, hearing, touching, tasting and smelling the objects around them. It is characterised by the absence of language. It is the conquest of objects stage.

Pre-Operational Stage (about 2 to 7 years): During this stage, children become better and better at using language to represent objects and events symbolically. Children use language not only to communicate with others but also to communicate with themselves, talking around or silently (that is thinking). In this stage, the children seem to identify objects by their names and put them into certain classes. However, they usually make mistakes in this proves of identification and concept formation.

Their mode of thinking and reasoning is quite illogical at this stage. It is neither inductive nor deductive but rather transductive in nature. Their thinking is sometimes too imaginative and for removed from reality. At this stage they are unable to distinguish between living and non-living objects. (for them the doll in their hands is a live baby who can cry, smile and sleep). At this stage the intellectual structure of the child is concerned with his egocentric nature. By egocentric Piaget means that the child can see the world only from his own standpoint (S/he considers that the sun and moon are following him). The most striking characteristic of pre-operational thinking is the absence of adult forms of logic. Children begin to use adult logic when they progress to the concrete operations stage.

Concrete Operational Stage (From 7 to 11years): Consequently, children remain at the concrete operational stage of cognitive development during most of elementary school. Elementary school students begin to use adult forms of logic, but they can apply their new-found logic only to concrete situations. They can think logically about things they can experience, but not about hypothetical situations. They begin to think in terms of a set of interrelated principles rather than single bits of knowledge. As a result they can think in terms of systems.

Their thinking becomes more logical and systematic. They can now make use of inductive and deductive approaches in terms of reasoning and arriving at conclusions. The child now develops the ability to conserve both in terms of quantity and number of objects. S/he can now very well think the change in appearance of an object does not alter either its quantity or its number. The think of the child is no longer 'rigid' and irreversible. A female child who has a sister now clearly realises that her sister also has a sister.

The child is no longer ego-centric in his thinking. At this stage the child can classify the objects. He develops the ability of serialisation like arranging things from largest to smallest and vice versa. The child now learns to carry out rather complex operations or tackle problems as long as they are concrete and not abstract.

Formal Operational Stage (From 11 and onwards): Concrete operational children can apply logic only to "here and now" situations. People in the formal operations stage can apply logic to abstract and hypothetical situations. Formal thinking requires the ability to think abstractly. Works of literature and art can take on abstract meaning only to someone in formal operations. Formal operational thinkers can also engage in hypotheses testing, or scientific thinking.

Generalisations and framing of rules by operating in abstract terms become quite possible at this stage. Formal operations thinker begins to look at problems in many ways and explore various solutions but in a very systematic and logical way. The four stages of cognitive development coincide with approximate age ranges and characteristics.

Educational implication

- — Piaget's theory has highlighted the importance of drives and motivation in the field of learning and development.
- — This theory provides valuable information and advice on curriculum planning and structuring the schemes of studies.
- — It may provide a suitable framework of the learning experiences in view of the cognitive development of the learner and the needs of society.
- — The knowledge of Piaget's theory may prove quite valuable to teachers and parents for making them aware of the nature of the thought processes of the children at a particular level of maturation or chronological age.
- — This theory gives the idea that learning experience should be linked and related with one's old learning so that they may be reasonably easy for being assimilated and understood by the learner.
- — It has placed a major responsibility on parents, teachers and other directly or indirectly connected with the education and welfare of children to arrange for the most appropriate and stimulating environment for their children.
- — It emphasises on the individualisation of education.
- — It stresses the importance of the variety of aid material other than verbal communication.

Gagne theory

Rober M. Gangne is a prominent educational psychologist who has developed a behavioistic eclectic approach to the psychology of learning. Gagne's conceptual model is an information processing theory with in which man's learning processes are taken to be analogous to the operations of a computer. He presented the conditions of learning. His theory is used to underpin the mechanistic instructional technology that is associated with behaviour modification and performance or competencybased education.

For Gagne the purpose of psychology is to observe conditions under which learning occurs and to describe them in objective terms. In his view, learner's senses, nervous system and mussels are important aspects in learning process. They work as instrument condition. Instrumental conditioning is largely a matter of information processing, within this process, learning as a total process begins with a phase of apprehending the stimulus situation. Proceeds to the stage of acquisition, then to storage and finally to retrieval. Learning of any new capability requires the prior learning of the subordinate capabilities that are involved in the new capability.

Robert Gagne's Five Major Domains of Learning Outcomes

Outcomes of learning (major domains)	Examples	Suggested conditions for facilitating outcomes
1. Intellectual skills Problem solving (Higher-order rules) optimal order of topics	Learner determines in an instructional sequence through experimentation.	Review of relevant rules; verbal instructions to aid in recall of rules; verbal instructions to direct thought processes
Rules	Learner demonstrates that metals expand	Learner is made aware of desired

	when heated and contract when cooled.	learning outcome; review of relevant concepts; concrete examples.
Concepts	Learner classifies objects in terms of size, shape, function, position, colour.	Examples presented; learner actively involved in finding examples; reinforcement.
Discriminations	Learner distinguishes among various printed letters of the alphabet.	Simultaneous presentation of stimuli to be discriminated; reinforcement (confirmation); repetition.
2. Verbal information	Learner recalls information in writing or orally.	Advance organisers; meaningful context; instructional aids for motivation and retention.
3. Cognitive strategies	Learner devises personal strategy for remembering complex verbal material	Frequent presentation of novel and/or challenging problems
4. Attitudes	Learner selects among a choice of activities (subject, teacher, schools)	Models; reinforcement; verbal guidance
5. Motor skills	Learner types (swims,walks, runs, flies).	Model: verbal directions; reinforcement (knowledge of results); practice.

Gagne classifies human capabilities into five major domains. Those are the outcomes of learning;

Intellectual Skills: These are hierarchically arranged in the sense that higher-level skills depend upon lower-level skills. These include the learning of discriminations, rules and concepts.

Verbal Information: It consists of a student's merely stating the desired information.

Cognitive Strategies: These are a special kind of intellectual skill that pertains to the behaviour of a learner, regardless of what s/he is studying. Cognitive skills are what we actually do when we learn, think, and remember-rehearsing of elaborating.

Attitudes: Attitudes are acquired internal states of organisms that influence their actions toward certain class of things, persons or events. Persons in activities such as driving a car playing a musical instrument employ motor skills.

2

EDUCATIONAL PSYCHOLOGY AS A FOUNDATION

Teaching educational psychology to cohorts of students in teacher education might facilitate the development of shared knowledge and experiences related to educational psychology by students in the cohort. In addition, this cohort structure might encourage social interaction of the type that has been found to be effective in developing critical thinking strategies and problem solving in children. Theory and research suggest that meaningful learning and application of educational psychology might be facilitated by closer collaboration between educational psychologists, teacher educators, and subject matter researchers.

But the reward structure for faculty in research universities will need to change both to promote closer collaboration between these educators and researchers and also to encourage faculty to spend time and effort on working to design innovative approaches to teaching educational psychology in the context of teacher education within real classrooms and schools. If we are to advance in our knowledge of the learning of educational psychology as a discipline, then we need to apply methods similar to those used to study childrens' knowledge and cognition to the study of learning by students in teacher education.

The way in which teachers are educated and supported to meet the challenges of the 21st century has become a contended issue. In raising alarm, criticising the status quo, and making recommendations, various study groups and blue ribbon panels have focussed on economic issues, equity and excellence, the need for more rigorous subject matter preparation, and on the restructuring of incentives and the career ladder for teachers. Although considerable agreement exists about the need for improvement in teacher education and professional development, wide differences of opinion are apparent about where to concentrate limited resources. These differences of opinion will probably persist as the recommendations and mandates of the 1980s become the legislation, regulations, and redesigned teacher preparation programmes of the 1990s.

But whatever programmes and designs emerge from the present period of scrutiny, research, and revision in teacher education, we are confident that each route to certification will include substantial attention to learners, learning, and human development. For, in the broadest sense, the roles and purposes of teachers will continue to focus on the facilitation of learning and development by each student, to the practical limits of teachers' abilities. Consider what one portrait of future teachers implies about their knowledge of learning and development.

Such teachers would possess broad and deep understanding of children, the subjects they teach, the nature of learning and schooling, and the world around them. They exemplify the critical thinking they strive to develop in students, combining tough-minded instruction with a penchant for inquiry. Competent teachers are careful not to bore, confuse, or demean students, pushing them instead to interact with important knowledge and skill. Such teachers interpret the understandings that students bring to and develop during lessons; they identify students' misconceptions, and question their surface responses that mask true learning.

A teacher who has deep knowledge of the psychology of learning, development, and instruction; who is able to apply and draw on this psychological knowledge in her own teaching; who is able to transform this knowledge when necessary to adapt to new learning situations and learners; and who is continuously adding to and developing psychological knowledge through informal inquiry, as well as through formal education. Thus, knowledge of the domain of educational psychology is central to the teaching enterprise and to the preparation of teachers.

It was less than a century ago that William James, in his Talks to Teachers, made the argument for including psychology in the preparation of teachers. At that time, psychology was an infant science with only the sketchiest understanding of the human learner and human cognition. Since then, educational psychologists have filled in much detail in the explanation of human cognition that James put forth:

The gist of the matter is this: Every impression that comes in from without, be it a sentence which we hear, an object of vision, or an effluvium which assails our nose, no sooner enters our consciousness than it is drafted off in some determinate direction or other, making connection with the other materials already there, and finally producing what we call our reaction. The impression arouses its old associates; they go out to meet it; it is received by them, recognised by the mind. It is the fate of every impression thus to fall into a mind preoccupied with memories, ideas, and interests, and by these it is taken in. This way of taking in the object is the process of apperception. The apperceived impression is engulfed in this, and the result is a new field of consciousness, of which one part comes from the outer world, and another part comes from the previous contents of the mind.

Although James' vision of the learner anticipated much of the work by contemporary educational psychologists on cognition and instruction, today educational psychologists have more to contribute to the teaching-learning enterprise than they did a century ago. For example, in the last decade research on learning has revealed a great deal about students' conceptions and misconceptions and has shown how the knowledge that students bring to the teaching-learning situation affects substantially what and how students learn.

William James' broad and general claims about learning have been supported and elaborated by subject-matter specific research on teaching and school learning. Although one prominent source of proposals for reform of teacher preparation, the Holmes Group, drew significantly on recent theory and research in the psychology of learning and teaching in portraying the ideal teacher, their report left the re-formulation of educational psychology as a course of study undefined.

The Group's only caveat was that "professional courses of study in education should meet the standards of the core disciplines from which they derive; that is educational psychology must be sound psychology." Now that many institutions are attempting to build on such general recommendations to reform their teacher education programmes, faculty need to begin to explicate, more specifically, the learning and teaching of educational psychology in the preparation of teachers for the 21st century.

EDUCATIONAL PSYCHOLOGY IN NEW TEACHER PREPARATION PROGRAMMES

A growing awareness among educational psychologists of

the need to re-examine their own discipline. Such a re-examination needs to focus not only on the learning and teaching of educational psychology but also on understanding how educational psychology as a course of study influences the knowledge of candidates in teacher preparation. The content and methods of educational psychology courses seem to be determined largely by the scope and sequence of educational psychology textbooks, which seem to reflect a static conception of educational psychology as a "foundation" in teacher education.

Learning and Teaching

What emerged was not a new "scope and sequence chart" for the teaching of educational psychology, but rather several interconnected questions and problems that might provoke our thinking and some researchers begin to consider how educational psychology should be incorporated into revised teacher education programmes. Each suggests inherent dilemmas for the learning and teaching of educational psychology. Some of these dilemmas may be resolved or managed by appeal to empirical research on teaching and learning. Others may yield to practical constraints or to local traditions, norms, and preferences.

In any case, as educational psychologists, to engage in thoughtful dialogue about what knowledge our field has to offer to future teachers and how that knowledge might be taught well. The questions confront both educational psychologists and teacher educators with four persisting problems of practice in preparing professionals for a changing profession: the problem of transfer or application of psychological knowledge, the problem of balance between general and content specific knowledge about school learning, the need to consider the knowledge and beliefs of prospective teachers, and the challenge of applying knowledge about teachers' learning to the teaching and learning of educational psychology.

In short, the curriculum and the instructional approaches appropriate for creating an educational psychology for teachers in tomorrow's schools need examination in light of recent research on teaching and learning. In what follows, these problems use to frame a discussion of issues to be considered in rethinking educational psychology as a foundation in teacher education.

TRANSFER PROBLEM

Educational psychology is taught as a foundation course in most teacher education programmes, and at least one course on the psychology of human learning is typically required for teacher certification by most states. Typically, in most colleges and universities teacher education majors take a course or courses in the psychology of learning, development, and instruction prior to taking their methods courses, practicum experiences, and to doing their actual teaching in schools. The pattern, sequencing, and methods of teaching educational psychology make implicit assumptions about teachers' knowledge about learners and learning.

An underlying rationale for the timing and format of educational psychology courses is that teacher education majors need the basic factual information and conceptual knowledge of the psychology of learning, development, and instruction to be able to apply this knowledge in their clinical teaching experiences, in their methods courses, and, eventually, in their classroom teaching. Thus, the teaching of educational psychology as a foundation in teacher education has rested on certain classic but typically, unquestioned, psychological assumptions about the learning and the transfer of learning of the prospective teacher to teaching.

From early attempts to extrapolate laws of learning from laboratory studies of animal learning to the present writers of contemporary educational psychology textbooks who still harken back to some "rather obvious principles known since the beginning of this century," educational psychologists have framed the problem as one of transfer of learning from one situation to another, or from in school to out of school. R.M.Gagné introduced the concepts of vertical transfer and horizontal transfer-two concepts that have affected significantly the content and methods of teaching educational psychology for the past two decades. In his theory of vertical transfer, Gagné posited the idea that learning of lower level skills in a learning hierarchy facilitates the learning of higher level skills in the hierarchy because they serve as prerequisites for those higher level skills as follows:

> In vertical transfer, intellectual skills exhibit transfer to "higher-level" skills, that is, to skills which are more complex. The intellectual skill of multiplying whole numbers, for example, is a part of the more complex skills of dividing, adding, and multiplying fractions, finding square roots, solving proportions, and many others. Transfer to the learning of these more complex skills is dependent primarily on the prior learning of the simpler skills. The more basic skills must be "mastered," in the sense that they can be readily retrieved, in order for transfer to take place to the learning of the more complex intellectual skills. This principle is illustrated by the learning hierarchy.

While Gagné's description of vertical transfer seems to pertain more to the learner's procedural knowledge, Bloom et. al's Taxonomy of Educational Objectives sets forth a similar hierarchical model with the application of factual knowledge being dependent on prior learning of propositional knowledge and factual information. Thus, in an educational psychology course the prospective teacher might be taught the "definition of learning" prior to being taught the "principle of learning" on the assumption that the propositional knowledge-the definition-is necessary to learn the principle. Gagné identified a second kind of transfer as lateral or horizontal transfer. He defined lateral transfer as generalisation by the learner of what is learned in one situation to a new situation that differs from the situation in which the learning occurred.

An example of lateral transfer in teaching would be learning a principle of child development in an educational psychology course and then applying that principle in teaching practice. Gagné argued that "There is evidently some advantage to having the learner practice the application of the skill to a variety of situations or problem contexts." By implication there must exist a knowledge base in educational psychology, including psychological facts, principles, and theories, of learning, development, and learners that the teacher education student would learn and then would be able to apply and transfer to the actual teaching situation.

In some ways, this dilemma is similar to that posed in the design of curricula for learning and teaching of reading and mathematics in elementary schools. In the past, most teaching in elementary reading and mathematics has rested on the assumption, derived primarily from task analyses and behavioural psychology, that students must learn the lower order facts and skills before going on to master higher order problem solving and application skills.

In contrast, recent theory and research from cognitive psychology call this idea into question: This assumption-that there is a sequence from lower level activities that do not require much independent thinking or judgment to higher level ones that do-colors much educational theory and practice. Implicitly at least, it justifies long years of drill on the "basics" before thinking and problem solving are demanded. Cognitive research on the nature of basic skills such as reading and mathematics provides a fundamental challenge to this assumption.

For example, computational skills may not exist as lower order prerequisites for higher order mathematical problem solving, but rather are learned in relation to, and as part of, the problem solving activity. Ample evidence also exists that both top-down and bottom-up processes are involved in reading. An important point is that new information to be learned and taught needs to be related in a meaningful way to knowledge and information that the learner already knows. Thus, instructional content and practices ought to relate new knowledge in a meaningful way to the knowledge that students have already developed. This means, for example, that reading should be taught with a basis in meaning and that mathematics computation should be taught in the context of problem solving.

What does this rethinking of elementary reading and arithmetic teaching and learning imply about educational psychology for prospective teachers? If learning involves both top-down and bottom-up processes, then a hierarchical model in which educational psychology is a prerequisite or a foundation in teacher education is inconsistent with the best psychological research and theory. Researchers are also questioning the notion of horizontal transfer and the relationship of inschool and out-of-school learning. For example, researchers have discovered instances where students have learned and can perform complicated mathematical procedures with understanding in an out-of-school setting.

In contrast, mathematical procedures that students learn in school often do not transfer to the out-of-school setting. This notion of knowledge as contextually situated calls into question the basic notions of how to facilitate learning in school being used and applied later by the student in real-life situations. Although concepts of vertical and horizontal transfer have affected the teaching of educational psychology as a foundation for at least two decades, we need to reconsider them as well as the content and methods of educational psychology in light of several alternative framing assumptions that have emerged from recent research on cognition and instruction. These include the notions that thinking and cognition are situated in physical and social contexts, that thinking and learning are situated within the contexts of personal and social epistemologies, beliefs, and understandings; and that learners have "strong potential capabilities for cognitive growth that enable complex and subtle processes of construction of knowledge and thinking skills."

These alternative framing assumptions are related not only to the substance of what is traditionally taught and learned, but also to the methods by which learning is presumed to take place. Given these alternative framing assumptions, researchers have begun to think differently about knowledge and about the thinking and learning of children and youth in school and out. Just as we are beginning to think differently about the development of children's knowledge and about the learning and thinking of children, we may also need to begin to think differently about the development of teachers' knowledge about learners, learning, and development and about how we facilitate the learning and thinking of teachers through teacher education. In doing so, we need to consider how these alternative framing assumptions fit with our developing understanding of the psychology of teachers' knowledge and thinking and the contextualised nature of that knowledge and thinking.

Teachers' General and Subject-matter-embedded Knowledge of Learning

An important beginning question is how to think about teachers' knowledge of the principles and theories of learning and development that define much of the domain of knowledge in educational psychology that is relevant to teachers. Such knowledge is what comprises most of the texts currently used in educational psychology courses for teachers. It includes what Shulman has referred to as knowledge of learners and their characteristics-as well as aspects of what he has identified as pedagogical content knowledge.

The conceptual and procedural knowledge that students bring to the learning of a topic, the misconceptions they may have developed, and the stages of understanding that they are likely to pass through in moving from a state of having little understanding of the topic to mastery of it. It also includes knowledge of techniques for assessing students' understandings and diagnosing their misconceptions.

The above knowledge clearly concerns the psychology of learning even though it is embedded within a specific subject or content area. Relevant knowledge also includes teachers' content-specific cognitional knowledge or teachers' awareness of the mental processes or cognitions by which learners acquire subject-specific knowledge through classroom learning. To illustrate a possible way in which educational psychologists might think differently about the knowledge that teachers need to develop about the psychology of learning, here use as an example from recent research that Peterson conducted with her colleagues Thomas Carpenter and Elizabeth Fennema at the University of Wisconsin-Madison. Here researchers tried to make accessible to teachers some knowledge from psychological research on children's learning of addition and subtraction. Because recent research had shown the importance of initial knowledge, researchers began by asking to what extent teachers already have this knowledge:

a) What do teachers know about the distinctions that young learners naturally make between addition and subtraction problems types? and
b) What do teachers know about the strategies that children use to solve different addition and subtraction word problems?

They assessed teachers' knowledge through questionnaires and an interview and found that, in general, most of the 40 first-grade teachers were able to identify many of the critical distinctions between addition and subtraction word problems and the primary strategies that children use to solve such problems. However, teachers' knowledge generally was not organised into a coherent network that related distinctions between problems, children's strategies, children's solutions, and problem difficulty. Given that it took many years of research for psychologists to arrive at such knowledge, perhaps it is not surprising that teachers did not have this in-depth and coherent network of knowledge of young childrens' learning of addition and subtraction.

In a subsequent experimental portion of the study researchers showed that by working with these teachers and giving them access to recent research knowledge from on childrens' thinking processes in learning addition and subtraction, the teachers' knowledge base was enhanced. Rather than teaching addition and subtraction facts and computations, experimental teachers taught addition and subtraction within the context of story problems. Experimental group teachers were more knowledgeable about childrens' learning processes than control teachers who had not participated in the workshop.

By observing these teachers in their classrooms during the following year, researchers found that experimental teachers were able to use this knowledge to assess their childrens' thinking and to modify their instruction in addition and subtraction. Children in experimental teachers' classes were better at solving complex addition and subtraction story problems than were children in control teachers' classes and were more confident of their ability to do so. Children in experimental teachers classes also knew the addition and subtraction facts as well as did children in control teachers' classes.

These research findings have two implications for the knowledge of educational psychology that is relevant to teachers. First, the research demonstrates that there is new, emerging knowledge of the psychology of children's learning of mathematics. By being given access to this knowledge, teachers modified their knowledge and understanding of children's mathematics learning, changed their classroom instruction, and improved their childrens' mathematics problem solving and learning of number facts. The research demonstrates the importance of contextualised or situated knowledge of the psychology of childrens' learning to the continuing education of teachers who are then able to facilitate the meaningful learning, understanding, and problem solving of their students.

Left for further thought and discussion is the question of how to provide such integrated knowledge and practice in the education of prospective teachers who typically do not have daily access to teaching young learners and who typically do not learn educational psychology within the context of their actual teaching. Second, the findings suggest a possible evolution in the boundaries of the domain of educational psychology that is relevant to teachers. According to this conception, educational psychology would include subject-matter-embedded knowledge of the psychology of learning and development, as well as more general knowledge of theories of learning and development.

A related implication is that in teaching educational psychology, educational psychologists need to work more closely with subject matter specialists, just as they have in the development of this knowledge through research. Although the above discussion refers to the psychology of learning mathematics, the same argument might be applied to other subject areas, for example, reading and science. Third, the research of Peterson and her colleagues was based on the idea that children's learning of addition and subtraction is a process of active construction of knowledge. In working with the teachers they took the same view of teachers' learning as a process of active construction of knowledge.

TEACHERS' LEARNING AS ACTIVE CONSTRUCTION OF KNOWLEDGE

Over the past decade, educational psychologists studying children's learning and cognition have provided extensive evidence that "problem solving, comprehension, and learning are based on knowledge, and that people continually try to understand and think about the new in terms of what they already know." More and more psychologists are viewing learning as a process of active construction of knowledge by the learner. Such a constructivist view of learning stands in sharp contrast to passive reception or absorption psychological models of learning that have dominated educational practice for decades.

Although researchers have done some cognitive analyses of the subject matter knowledge of teachers, they have not yet done similar cognitive analyses of the prior knowledge and learning of educational psychology by teachers. Such research might be conducted to understand how students in teacher education come to construct knowledge actively in the domain of educational psychology.

In addition to the assumption of learning as active construction of knowledge psychologists have proposed, as a framing assumption, that thinking and learning are situated in contexts of beliefs and understandings about cognition. Thus, for example, a teacher's learning is situated within the context of her beliefs and understandings of what she considers knowledge and understandings to be. In the work with first-grade teachers, researchers viewed the staff development workshop with teachers as only the beginning of a process of knowledge construction and learning for the teachers. During the workshop, teachers viewed videotapes of actual children solving problems in addition and subtraction. Then each teacher interviewed a child, gave the child different types of word problems, and then asked the child how he or she solved the problem.

Thus, beginning in the workshop, the teachers gathered evidence and tested for themselves to ascertain that children entering first-grade do have knowledge and strategies for solving word problems. When teachers began teaching addition and subtraction to their own classes, they further tested these ideas with their own students. During the summer when viewing the videotapes, many teachers regarded some of the videotaped children as exceptional and were skeptical childrens' informal knowledge and abilities to solve certain kinds of problems. However, when teachers began posing problems to their own students in the fall and, listening carefully, and seeing for themselves their own students' abilities to solve problems, they found out that the children they had seen on the videotapes during the workshop were not exceptional and that their children had knowledge and strategies for solving many types of word problems.

Teachers came to see that children can solve different problems by counting or modeling the quantities and relationships between the quantities and the problem with physical objects. This knowledge then served as a "hook" into expanding teachers' understanding of children's informal and formal mathematical knowledge and thinking. Teachers' beliefs about children's knowledge changed most fundamentally as a result of asking kids to solve word problems aloud during class and then listening to the strategies that children use to solve those problems. The teachers who became most knowledgeable about their own students' mathematics knowledge and strategies in solving word problems and who also held most constructively oriented beliefs about childrens' knowledge tended to adopt a personal and active constructivist view of the learning process and of childrens' mathematics understanding.

Teachers who experienced the workshop differed in the extent to which they knew and believed that children enter first grade with useful problem-solving knowledge. Some teachers clearly knew and believed that children have their own knowledge. These teachers were taking seriously the processes the children use to solve problems and were attending to the knowledge that their students had. The growth of teachers knowledge demonstrates the development of thoughtful teaching of the kind portrayed in recent reform reports.

PSYCHOLOGY OF TEACHERS' LEARNING

If teachers are to become thoughtful professionals, they need to have both meta cognitive knowledge for classroom learning as well as meta cognitive knowledge for classroom teaching. The former involves learners' self-awareness of their own cognitions through which they acquire information, gain understanding, and learn in the classroom. Metacognitive knowledge for classroom teaching includes self-awareness and ability to reflect on one's own cognitive knowledge for classroom learning, as well as ability to reflect on knowledge about classroom teaching. Although little research has been done on such metacognitive knowledge of teachers, many researchers, including educational psychologists, are now suggesting that teachers' self-awareness and deliberate action are important aspects of teaching expertise that need to be studied.

Here illustrates the centrality of knowledge of the psychology of teachers' learning. There are three points for consideration: first, that the psychology of teachers' learning constitutes an important new domain of knowledge in educational psychology; second, that the knowledge of theories and research findings on the psychology of teachers' learning may be meaningful and important for students in teacher education, and further, may enhance their teaching practice; and finally, that knowledge of the psychology of teachers' learning may enhance the ability of faculty to teach educational psychology more effectively in teacher preparation programmes.

Educational psychology has contributed to the preparation of teachers for at least the last century through courses, texts, and teaching/testing materials. The relationship between educational psychology and teacher education has changed over time as educational psychology moved from a body of theory derived in laboratories that was assumed to apply to teaching to a field that directly studies many problems and tasks of classroom and subject matter teaching and learning. The content of educational psychology for teachers has also expanded to include not only the characteristics of learners and the processes of learning, but also settings and formats for teaching.

Several current research endeavors suggest the emergence of a new domain of knowledge in educational psychology—the psychology of teachers' learning. Knowledge of the psychology of teachers' learning might contribute to the effective teaching of educational psychology in two ways:

— First, such knowledge would be useful as educational psychologists begin the process of conceptualising the learning and teaching of educational psychology in the preparation of teachers for the 21st century.

— Second, such knowledge would be particularly informative as educational psychologists think about the possibility of adapting the content and methods of educational psychology to the individual learner.

ADAPTATION OF CONTENT AND METHODS OF EDUCATIONAL PSYCHOLOGY

A final question concerns how to adapt the content and methods of educational psychology to the individual learner-the teacher-to facilitate the meaningful learning and application of that learning to teaching practice. Although some deeply entrenched notions of transfer have dominated the teaching of educational psychology for two decades, recent research on cognition and instruction suggests the need to think differently about it. For example, if cognitive research suggests that first graders come to know and understand addition and subtraction best within the context of a real-world story problem relevant to their lives, then the teacher should begin with the story problem to teach the addition/ subtraction number facts and problem solving.

The student is simultaneously learning number facts while solving a story problem. Similarly, the story or word problem (which would have previously been conceptualised as a transfer or application activity) serves as the context for learning computation and problem solving (which would previously have been thought of as the in-school skill.) The use of word problems as the context for children's learning of addition and subtraction has come from years of comprehensive research on children's learning of addition and subtraction. Unfortunately, similar research has not yet been done on teachers' meaningful learning and application of educational psychology.

Recent work on everyday learning, learning outside of school, and the contextualisation of cognitive tasks has demonstrated the importance of context in affecting meaningful learning, task performance, and application to a work environment. Thus, we can only speculate and propose the following for consideration: Just as childrens' meaningful learning and application of mathematics skills is facilitated by teaching-learning within the context of real-life mathematics problems, teachers' meaningful learning and application of knowledge and theories in educational psychology may be facilitated by teaching and learning educational psychology within the context of real-life teaching-learning problems or cases.

Recently, some educational psychologists have suggested that the study of cases may serve as a basis for meaningful learning and teaching in teacher education. Cases have long been used effectively in the education of lawyers as well as physicians.

Case for Cases

In the context of the learning and teaching of educational

psychology, a case might represent a realistic learning-teaching problem in a classroom. Thus, such cases for teachers in educational psychology would be similar to the real-life story problem experience of the first grader learning addition and subtraction.

Cases might take the form of print, text, video or audio recordings, jointly witnessed field experiences, or role-played simulations of a learning-teaching problem. Although the advocates for use of cases are increasing, some scholars are more cautious and are urging systematic study and analyses of how to facilitate students' knowledge growth and learning from cases. Use of cases was particularly effective in the context of the learning and teaching of strategies aimed at reflective decision making. Preservice teachers were encouraged to develop their own teaching schemata or representations for classroom management. Self-questions, inner-directed speech, and examples of reflective processes were provided to scaffold the teachers' development of their own representations of classroom management. Cases were used in two ways:

1. First, cases were used in the context of decision making training. In this situation class members worked in pairs, and each pair member read a vignette about a classroom management situation that ended with a problem or dilemma. One member was instructed to act as a reflective decision maker who reported decision-making thought processes while the other acted as observer who critiqued her/his partner's reflective processing. Cases were also used by the instructor to lead discussions aimed at guiding participants to use specified reflective decision making processes to analyse a depicted teacher's handling of a classroom management event.

2. In another approach (the technical skills approach), the cases were used to teach and

> illustrate technical principles of classroom management derived from research by educational psychologists. Although teachers who experienced reflective decision making were not taught technical principles, they knew these principles of classroom management by the end of the course as well as did students in the technical principle group. Also, in contrast to students who learned the technical skills approach, students taught the reflective approach showed better understanding and processing of classroom situations when confronted with a videotaped case that posed a real classroom management dilemma. The learning and teaching orientation in the reflective decision-making approach did more to facilitate sophisticated cognitive processing and thinking by the preservice teachers than did the orientation in the technical skills approach.

Cases provide a mechanism for shared thinking and construction knowledge in a group situation. Each student in educational psychology will see the same case differently because each brings different knowledge and beliefs to the experience. Thus, students in educational psychology, even when viewing or reading the same case, will construe the case or think about it in terms of their past and current teaching-learning experiences. Sharing of individuals' thinking about cases and arguing and justifying different interpretations may be particularly powerful ways of promoting thinking and reflection in prospective teachers.

Moreover, individual cases might be selected and tailored to individual students of educational psychology. Although adaptation to the individual learner has long been advocated by educational psychologists, the development and use of educational psychological knowledge by students in teacher education may depend on educational psychologists listening to their own advice.

Problem of Adaptation

Facilitation of transfer is often a reason for adapting content and methods of educational psychology to the individual learner. If the content and methods of educational psychology were adapted completely to the needs of the individual student in teacher education, the student would have little work to do to transfer or transform the information and content of educational psychology in order to learn and apply educational psychology to teaching. Cognitive research has demonstrated that specific subject matter knowledge plays an important role in learning and thinking. Thus, for the ninth grade mathematics teacher, at least part of the content and methods of educational psychology needs to focus on learning and teaching of mathematics in ninth grade. However, the ninth-grade math teacher also needs to understand more general issues of learning and development.

In teaching educational psychology, educational psychologists are faced with a fundamental dilemma: whether to offer an educational psychology that is primarily concerned with prospective teachers' own learning and development, or one that is primarily concerned with the learning and development of school children. Prospective teachers are adult learners and should be taught as adults. But they need to learn and know theories of learning and development relevant to the children and youth they will teach. A teacher-as-adult-learner approach to educational psychology would have educational psychologists teach in ways consistent with the learning and teaching processes that beginning teachers themselves should use in their classrooms.

Possibly, even if teaching and learning are situated or domain-specific, teachers will deduce some principles from their adult learning experiences and will apply these principles to the actual situation in which they would teach. Many constructivist approaches to working with teachers begin by having the inservice or preservice teachers work on learning tasks or solve problems themselves. Out of these experiences and insights into their own thinking and learning, teachers develop beliefs and understandings about cognition that may carry over to the way they think about the knowledge and understanding of their children as they teach.

Alternatively, a psychology-of-young-learners approach suggests that students of educational psychology should study content and methods dealing primarily with specific children and school situations to be later encountered on the job. This second approach runs the risk of missing the mark when teachers find themselves working with students and in situations that differ in important ways from those they experienced during teacher preparation. The problem of transfer and adaptation to the individual learner and teaching situation remains a fundamental dilemma that faculty need to consider as they conceptualise educational psychology in the new teacher preparation programmes.

3

LEARNING TO READ AND WRITE

Learning to read and write is critical to a child's success in school and later in life. One of the best predictors of whether a child will function competently in school and go on to contribute actively in our increasingly literate society is the level to which the child progresses in reading and writing. Although reading and writing abilities continue to develop throughout the life span, the early childhood years-from birth through age eight-are the most important period for literacy development. The statement consists of a set of principles and recomme-ndations for teaching practices and public policy.

The primary purpose of this position statement is to provide guidance to teachers of young children in schools and early childhood programmes (including child care centers, preschools, and family child care homes) serving children from birth through age eight. By and large, the principles and practices suggested here also will be of interest to any adults who are in a position to influence a young child's learning and development-parents, grandparents, older siblings, tutors, and other community members. Teachers work in schools or programmes regulated by administrative policies as well as available resources.

Therefore secondary audiences for this position statement are school principals and programme administrators whose roles are critical in establishing a supportive climate for sound, developmentally appropriate teaching practices; and policymakers whose decisions determine whether adequate resources are available for high-quality early childhood education.

A great deal is known about how young children learn to read and write and how they can be helped toward literacy during the first five years of life. A great deal is known also about how to help children once compulsory schooling begins, whether in kindergarten or the primary grades. Today the definition of basic proficiency in literacy calls for a fairly high standard of reading comprehension and analysis.

The main reason is that literacy requirements of most jobs have increased significantly and are expected to increase further in the future. Communications that in the past were verbal now demand reading and writing-messages sent by electronic mail, Internet, or facsimile as well as print documents. With the increasing variation among young children in our programmes and schools, teaching today has become more challenging.

The children they teach today are more diverse in their backgrounds, experiences, and abilities than were those they taught in the past. Kindergarten classes now include children who have been in group settings for three or four years as well as children who are participating for the first time in an organised early childhood programme. Classes include both children with identified disabilities and children with exceptional abilities, children who are already independent readers and children who are just beginning to acquire some basic literacy knowledge and skills. Children in the group may speak different languages at varying levels of proficiency. Because of these individual and experiential variations, it is common to find within a kindergarten classroom a five-year range in children's literacy-related skills and functioning.

What this means is that some kindergartners may have skills characteristic of the typical threeyear-old, while others might be functioning at the level of the typical eight-year-old. Diversity is to be expected and embraced, but it can be overwhelming when teachers are expected to produce uniform outcomes for all, with no account taken of the initial range in abilities, experiences, interests, and personalities of individual children. Among many early childhood teachers, a maturationist view of young children's development persists despite much evidence to the contrary.

A readiness view of reading development assumes that there is a specific time in the early childhood years when the teaching of reading should begin. It also assumes that physical and neurological maturation alone prepare the child to take advantage of instruction in reading and writing. The readiness perspective implies that until children reach a certain stage of maturity all exposure to reading and writing, except perhaps being read stories, is a waste of time or even potentially harmful. Experiences throughout the early childhood years, birth through age eight, affect the development of literacy.

These experiences constantly interact with characteristics of individual children to determine the level of literacy skills a child ultimately achieves. Failing to give children literacy experiences until they are school age can severely limit the reading and writing levels they ultimately attain. Recognising the early beginnings of literacy acquisition too often has resulted in use of inappropriate teaching practices suited to older children or adults perhaps but ineffective with children in preschool, kindergarten, and the early grades.

Teaching practices associated with outdated views of literacy development and/or learning theories are still prevalent in many classrooms. Such practices include extensive whole-group instruction and intensive drill and practice on isolated skills for groups or individuals. These practices, not particularly effective for primary-grade children, are even less suitable and effective with preschool and kindergarten children.

Young children especially need to be engaged in experiences that make academic content meaningful and build on prior learning. It is vital for all children to have literacy experiences in schools and early childhood programmes. Such access is even more critical for children with limited home experiences in literacy. However, these school experiences must teach the broad range of language and literacy knowledge and skills to provide the solid foundation on which high levels of reading and writing ultimately depend.

Current policies and resources are inadequate in ensuring that preschool and primary teachers are qualified to support the literacy development of all children, a task requiring strong preservice preparation and ongoing professional development. For teachers of children younger than kindergarten age in the United States, no uniform preparation requirements or licensure standards exist. In fact, a high school diploma is the highest level of education required to be a child care teacher in most states.

Moreover, salaries in child care and preschool programmes are too low to attract or retain better qualified staff. Even in the primary grades, for which certified teachers are required, many states do not offer specialised early childhood certification, which means many teachers are not adequately prepared to teach reading and writing to young children.

All teachers of young children need good, foundational knowledge in language acquisition, including second-language learning, the processes of reading and writing, early literacy development, and experiences and teaching practices contributing to optimal develop-ment. Resources also are insufficient to ensure teachers continuing access to professional education so they can remain current in the field or can prepare to teach a different age group if they are reassigned.

Children take their first critical steps toward learning to read and write very early in life. Long before they can exhibit reading and writing production skills, they begin to acquire some basic understandings of the concepts about literacy and its functions. Children learn to use symbols, combining their oral language, pictures, print, and play into a coherent mixed medium and creating and communicating meanings in a variety of ways. From their initial experiences and interactions with adults, children begin to read words, processing letter-sound relations and acquiring substantial knowledge of the alphabetic system.

As they continue to learn, children increasingly consolidate this information into patterns that allow for automaticity and fluency in reading and writing. Consequently reading and writing acquisition is conceptualised better as a developmental continuum than as an all-or-nothing phenomenon. But the ability to read and write does not develop naturally, without careful planning and instruction. Children need regular and active interactions with print. Specific abilities required for reading and writing come from immediate experiences with oral and written language.

Experiences in these early years begin to define the assumptions and expectations about becoming literate and give children the motivation to work toward learning to read and write. From these experiences children learn that reading and writing are valuable tools that will help them do many things in life. Even in the first few months of life, children begin to experiment with language. Young babies make sounds that imitate the tones and rhythms of adult talk; they "read" gestures and facial expressions, and they begin to associate sound sequences frequently heard-words-with their referents.

They delight in listening to familiar jingles and rhymes, play along in games such as peek-a-boo and pat-a-cake, and manipulate objects such as board books and alphabet blocks in their play. From these remarkable beginnings children learn to use a variety of symbols. In the midst of gaining facility with these symbol systems, children acquire through interactions with others the insight that specific kinds of marks-print-also can represent meanings.

At first children will use the physical and visual cues surrounding print to determine what something says. But as they develop an understanding of the alphabetic principle, children begin to process letters, translate them into sounds, and connect this information with a known meaning. Although it may seem as though some children acquire these understandings magically or on their own, studies suggest that they are the beneficiaries of considerable, though playful and informal, adult guidance and instruction. Considerable diversity in children's oral and written language experiences occurs in these years. In home and child care situations, children encounter many different resources and types and degrees of support for early reading and writing.

Some children may have ready access to a range of writing and reading materials, while others may not; some children will observe their parents writing and reading frequently, others only occasionally; some children receive direct instruction, while others receive much more casual, informal assistance. What this means is that no one teaching method or approach is likely to be the most effective for all children. Rather, good teachers bring into play a variety of teaching strategies that can encompass the great diversity of children in schools.

Excellent instruction builds on what children already know, and can do, and provides knowledge, skills, and dispositions for lifelong learning. Children need to learn not only the technical skills of reading and writing but also how to use these tools to better their thinking and reasoning. The single most important activity for building these understandings and skills essential for reading success appears to be reading aloud to children.

High-quality book reading occurs when children feel emotionally secure and are active participants in reading. Asking predictive and analytic questions in smallgroup settings appears to affect children's vocabulary and comprehension of stories. Children may talk about the pictures, retell the story, discuss their favorite actions, and request multiple rereadings. It is the talk that surrounds the storybook reading that gives it power, helping children to bridge what is in the story and their own lives.

These types of conversations as "decontextualised language" in which teachers may induce higher-level thinking by moving experiences in stories from what the children may see in front of them to what they can imagine. A central goal during these preschool years is to enhance children's exposure to and concepts about print. Some teachers use Big Books to help children distinguish many print features, including the fact that print (rather than pictures) carries the meaning of the story, that the strings of letters between spaces are words and in print correspond to an oral version, and that reading progresses from left to right and top to bottom.

In the course of reading stories, teachers may demonstrate these features by pointing to individual words, directing children's attention to where to begin reading, and helping children to recognise letter shapes and sounds. The key to these critical concepts, such as developing word awareness, may lie in these demonstrations of how print works. Children also need opportunity to practice what they've learned about print with their peers and on their own. The physical arrangement of the classroom can promote time with books.

A key area is the classroom library-a collection of attractive stories and informational books that provides children with immediate access to books. Regular visits to the school or public library and library card registration ensure that children's collections remain continually updated and may help children develop the habit of reading as lifelong learning. In comfortable library settings children often will pretend to read, using visual cues to remember the words of their favorite stories. Although studies have shown that these pretend readings are just that, such visual readings may demonstrate substantial knowledge about the global features of reading and its purposes.

Story books are not the only means of providing children with exposure to written language. Children learn a lot about reading from the labels, signs, and other kinds of print, they see around them. Highly visible print labels on objects, signs, and bulletin boards in classrooms demonstrate the practical uses of written language. In environments rich with print, children incorporate literacy into their dramatic play, using these communication tools to enhance the drama and realism of the pretend situation. These everyday, playful experiences by themselves do not make most children readers.

Rather they expose children to a variety of print experiences and the processes of reading for real purposes. For children whose primary language is other than English, studies have shown that a strong basis in a first language promotes school achievement in a second language. Children who are learning English as a second language are more likely to become readers and writers of English when they are already familiar with the vocabulary and concepts in their primary language.

In this respect, oral and written language experiences should be regarded as an additive process, ensuring that children are able to maintain their home language while also learning to speak and read English. Including non-English materials and resources to the extent possible can help to support children's first language while children acquire oral proficiency in English. A fundamental insight developed in children's early years through instruction is the alphabetic principle, the understanding that there is a systematic relationship between letters and sounds.

The shapes of letters are learned by distinguishing one character from another by its type of spatial features. Teachers will often involve children in comparing letter shapes, helping them to differentiate a number of letters visually. Alphabet books and alphabet puzzles in which children can see and compare letters may be a key to efficient and easy learning. At the same time children learn about the sounds of language through exposure to linguistic awareness games, nursery rhymes, and rhythmic activities. Some research suggests that the roots of phonemic awareness, a powerful predictor of later reading success, are found in traditional rhyming, skipping, and word games. For example, researchers found that three-year-old children's knowledge of nursery rhymes specifically related to their more abstract phonological knowledge later on.

Engaging children in choral readings of rhymes and rhythms allows them to associate the symbols with the sounds they hear in these words. Although children's facility in phonemic awareness has been shown to be strongly related to later reading achievement, the precise role it plays in these early years is not fully understood. Phonemic awareness refers to a child's understanding and conscious awareness that speech is composed of identifiable units, such as spoken words, syllables, and sounds.

Training studies have demonstrated that phonemic awareness can be taught to children as young as age five. Linguistic games to engage children in explicitly manipulating speech segments at the phoneme level. Yet, whether such training is appropriate for younger-age children is highly suspect. Other scholars find that children benefit most from such training only after they have learned some letter names, shapes, and sounds and can apply what they learn to real reading in meaningful contexts.

Even at this later age, however, many children acquire phonemic awareness skills without specific training but as a consequence of learning to read. In the preschool years sensitising children to sound similarities does not seem to be strongly dependent on formal training but rather from listening to patterned, predictable texts while enjoying the feel of reading and language.

Children acquire a working knowledge of the alphabetic system not only through reading but also through writing. Even without formal spelling instruction, preschoolers use their tacit knowledge of phonological relations to spell words. Invented spelling (or phonic spelling) refers to beginners' use of the symbols they associate with the sounds they hear in the words they wish to write.

For example, a child may initially write b or bk for the word bike, to be followed by more conventionalised forms later on. Some educators may wonder whether invented spelling promotes poor spelling habits. To the contrary, studies suggest that temporary invented spelling may contribute to beginning reading. One study, for example, found that children benefited from using invented spelling compared to having the teacher provide correct spellings in writing.

Although children's invented spellings did not comply with correct spellings, the process encouraged them to think actively about letter-sound relations. As children engage in writing, they are learning to segment the words they wish to spell into constituent sounds. Classrooms that provide children with regular opportunities to express themselves on paper, without feeling too constrained for correct spelling and proper handwriting, also help children understand that writing has real purpose.

Teachers can organise situations that both demonstrate the writing process and get children actively involved in it. Some teachers serve as scribes and help children write down their ideas, keeping in mind the balance between children doing it themselves and asking for help. In the beginning these products likely emphasise pictures with few attempts at writing letters or words. With encouragement, children begin to label their pictures, tell stories, and attempt to write stories about the pictures they have drawn. Such novice writing activity sends the important message that writing is not just handwriting practice-children are using their own words to compose a message to communicate with others.

Thus the picture that emerges from research in these first years of children's reading and writing is one that emphasises wide exposure to print and to developing concepts about it and its forms and functions. Classrooms filled with print, language and literacy play, storybook reading, and writing allow children to experience the joy and power associated with reading and writing while mastering basic concepts about print that research has shown are strong predictors of achievement.

Learning and Teaching in Kindergarten

Knowledge of the forms and functions of print serves as a foundation from which children become increasingly sensitive to letter shapes, names, sounds, and words. However, not all children typically come to kindergarten with similar levels of knowledge about printed language. Estimating where each child is developmentally and building on that base, a key feature of all good teaching, is particularly important for the kindergarten teacher.

Instruction will need to be adapted to account for children's differences. For those children with lots of print experiences, instruction will extend their knowledge as they learn more about the formal features of letters and their sound correspondences. For other children with fewer prior experiences, initiating them to the alphabetic principle, that a limited set of letters comprises the alphabet and that these letters stand for the sounds that make up spoken words, will require more focused and direct instruction. In all cases, however, children need to interact with a rich variety of print.

In this critical year kindergarten teachers need to capitalise on every opportunity for enhancing children's vocabulary development. One approach is through listening to stories. Children need to be exposed to vocabulary from a wide variety of genres, including informational texts as well as narratives. The learning of vocabulary, however, is not necessarily simply a byproduct of reading stories. Some explanation of vocabulary words prior to listening to a story is related significantly to children's learning of new words.

Asking predictive and analytic questions before and after the readings produced positive effects on vocabulary and comprehension. Repeated readings appear to further reinforce the language of the text as well as to familiarise children with the way different genres are structured. Understanding the forms of informational and narrative texts seems to distinguish those children who have been well read to from those who have not. Pappas found that with multiple exposures to a story (three readings), children's retelling became increasingly rich, integrating what they knew about the world, the language of the book, and the message of the author.

Thus, considering the benefits for vocabulary development and comprehension, the case is strong for interactive storybook reading. Increasing the volume of children's playful, stimulating experiences with good books is associated with accelerated growth in reading competence. Activities that help children clarify the concept of word are also worthy of time and attention in the kindergarten curriculum. Language experience charts that let teachers demonstrate how talk can be written down provide a natural medium for children's developing word awareness in meaningful contexts.

Transposing children's spoken words into written symbols through dictation provides a concrete demonstration that strings of letters between spaces are words and that not all words are the same length. The value of what many teachers have known and done for years: Teacher dictations of children's stories help develop word awareness, spelling, and the conventions of written language. Many children enter kindergarten with at least some perfunctory knowledge of the alphabet letters. An important goal for the kindergarten teacher is to reinforce this skill by ensuring that children can recognise and discriminate these letter shapes with increasing ease and fluency.

Children's proficiency in letter naming is a wellestablished predictor of their end-of-year achievement, probably because it mediates the ability to remember sounds. Generally a good rule according to current learning theory is to start with the more easily visualised uppercase letters, to be followed by identifying lowercase letters. In each case, introducing just a few letters at a time, rather than many, enhances mastery. At about the time children are readily able to identify letter names, they begin to connect the letters with the sounds they hear. A fundamental insight in this phase of learning is that a letter and letter sequences map onto phonological forms. Phonemic awareness, however, is not merely a solitary insight or an instant ability.

Children who are phonemically aware can think about and manipulate sounds in words. They know when words rhyme or do not; they know when words begin or end with the same sound; and they know that a word like bat is composed of three sounds /b/ /a/ /t/ and that these sounds can be blended into a spoken word. Popular rhyming books, for example, may draw children's attention to rhyming patterns, serving as a basis for extending vocabulary. Using initial letter cues, children can learn many new words through analogy, taking the familiar word bake as a strategy for figuring out a new word, lake.

Further, as teachers engage children in shared writing, they can pause before writing a word, say it slowly, and stretch out the sounds as they write it. Such activities in the context of real reading and writing help children attend to the features of print and the alphabetic nature of English. There is accumulated evidence that instructing children in phonemic awareness activities in kindergarten enhances reading achievement. Although a large number of children will acquire phonemic awareness skills as they learn to read, an estimated 20% will not without additional training.

The long-term benefits of a carefully developed kindergarten curriculum that focused on word study and decoding skills, along with sets of stories so that children would be able to practice these skills in meaningful contexts. High school seniors who early on had received this type of instruction outperformed their counterparts on reading achievement, attitude toward schooling, grades, and attendance.

In kindergarten many children will begin to read some words through recognition or by processing letter-sound relations. Children's ability to read words is tied to their ability to write words in a somewhat reciprocal relationship. The more opportunities children have to write, the greater the likelihood that they will reproduce spellings of words they have seen and heard. To provide more intensive and extensive practice, some teachers try to integrate writing in other areas of the curriculum, like literacy-related play, and other project activities. These types of projects engage children in using reading and writing for multiple purposes while they are learning about topics meaningful to them.

Early literacy activities teach children a great deal about writing and reading but often in ways that do not look much like traditional elementary school instruction. Capitalising on the active and social nature of children's learning, early instruction must provide rich demonstrations, interactions, and models of literacy in the course of activities that make sense to young children. Children must also learn about the relation between oral and written language and the relation between letters, sounds, and words. In classrooms built around a wide variety of print activities, then in talking, reading, writing, playing, and listening to one another, children will want to read and write and feel capable that they can do so.

PRIMARY GRADES

Instruction takes on a more formal nature as children move into the elementary grades. Here it is virtually certain that children will receive at least some instruction from a commercially published product, like a basal or literature anthology series. Although research has clearly established that no one method is superior for all children, approaches that favor some type of systematic code instruction along with meaningful connected reading report children's superior progress in reading. Instruction should aim to teach the important letter-sound relationships, which once learned are practiced through having many opportunities to read.

As word recognition processes become more automatic, children are likely to allocate more attention to higher-level processes of comprehension. Since these reading experiences tend to be rewarding for children, they may read more often; thus reading achievement may be a by-product of reading enjoyment. One of the hallmarks of skilled reading is fluent, accurate word identification.

Yet instruction in simply word calling with flashcards is not reading. Real reading is comprehension. Children need to read a wide variety of interesting, comprehensible materials, which they can read orally with about 90 to 95% accuracy. In the beginning children are likely to read slowly and deliberately as they focus on exactly what's on the page. In fact they may seem "glued to print", figuring out the fine points of form at the word level.

However, children's reading expression, fluency, and comprehension generally improve when they read familiar texts. Some authorities have found the practice of repeated rereadings in which children reread short selections significantly enhances their confidence, fluency, and comprehension in reading. Children not only use their increasing knowledge of lettersound patterns to read unfamiliar texts. They also use a variety of strategies. Studies reveal that early readers are capable of being intentional in their use of metacognitive strategies.

Even in these early grades, children make predictions about what they are to read, self-correct, reread, and question if necessary, giving evidence that they are able to adjust their reading when understanding breaks down. But children also need time for independent practice. These activities may take on numerous forms. Some research, for example, has demonstrated the power ful effects that children's reading to their caregivers has on promoting confidence as well as reading proficiency.

Visiting the library and scheduling independent reading and writing periods in literacy-rich classrooms also provide children with opportunities to select books of their own choosing. They may engage in the social activities of reading with their peers, asking questions, and writing stories, all of which may nurture interest and appreciation for reading and writing. Supportive relationships between these communication processes lead many teachers to integrate reading and writing in classroom instruction.

After all, writing challenges children to actively think about print. As young authors struggle to express themselves, they come to grips with different written forms, syntactic patterns, and themes. They use writing for multiple purposes: to write descriptions, lists, and stories to communicate with others. It is important for teachers to expose children to a range of text forms, including stories, reports, and informational texts, and to help children select vocabulary and punctuate simple sentences that meet the demands of audience and purpose.

Since handwriting instruction helps children communicate effectively, it should also be part of the writing process. Short lessons demonstrating certain letter formations tied to the publication of writing provide an ideal time for instruction. Reading and writing workshops, in which teachers provide smallgroup and individual instruction, may help children to develop the skills they need for communicating with others. Although children's initial writing drafts will contain invented spellings, learning about spelling will take on increasing importance in these years.

Spelling instruction should be an important component of the reading and writing programme since it directly affects reading ability. Seeing a word in print, imagining how it is spelled, and copying new words is an effective way of acquiring spellings. Nevertheless, even though the teacher's goal is to foster more conventionalised forms, it is important to recognise that there is more to writing than just spelling and grammatically correct sentences. It is true that children will need adult help to master the complexities of the writing process. But they also will need to learn that the power of writing is expressing one's own ideas in ways that can be understood by others.

As children's capabilities develop and become more fluent, instruction will turn from a central focus on helping children learn to read and write to helping them read and write to learn. Increasingly the emphasis for teachers will be on encouraging children to become independent and productive readers, helping them to extend their reasoning and comprehension abilities in learning about their world. Teachers will need to provide challenging materials that require children to analyse and think creatively and from different points of view.

They also will need to ensure that children have practice in reading and writing (both in and out of school) and many opportunities to analyse topics, generate questions, and organise written responses for different purposes in meaningful activities. Throughout these critical years accurate assessment of children's knowledge, skills, and dispositions in reading and writing will help teachers better match instruction with how and what children are learning. However, early reading and writing cannot simply be measured as a set of narrowly-defined skills on standardised tests.

These measures often are not reliable or valid indicators of what children can do in typical practice, nor are they sensitive to language variation, culture, or the experiences of young children. Rather, a sound assessment should be anchored in real-life writing and reading tasks and continuously chronicle a wide range of children's literacy activities in different situations.

Good assessment is essential to help teachers tailor appropriate instruction to young children and to know when and how much intensive instruction on any particular skill or strategy might be needed. By the end of third grade, children will still have much to learn about literacy. Clearly some will be further along the path to independent reading and writing than others.

Yet with highquality instruction, the majority of children will be able to decode words with a fair degree of facility, use a variety of strategies to adapt to different types of text, and be able to communicate effectively for multiple purposes using conventionalised spelling and punctuation. Most of all they will have come to see themselves as capable readers and writers, having mastered the complex set of attitudes, expectations, behaviours, and skills related to written language.

Achieving high standards of literacy for every child a shared responsibility of schools, early childhood programmes, families, and communities. But teachers of young children, whether employed in preschools, child care programmes, or elementary schools, have a unique responsibility to promote children's literacy development, based on the most current professional knowledge and research.

A theoretical model of literacy learning and development as an interactive process. Research supports the view of the child as an active constructor of his or her own learning, while at the same time studies emphasise the critical role of the supportive, interested, engaged adult (e.g., teacher, parent, or tutor) who provides scaffolding for the child's development of greater skill and understanding.

The principle of learning is that "children are active learners, drawing on direct social and physical experience as well as culturally transmitted knowledge to construct their own understandings of the world around them". Goals and expectations for young children's achievement in reading and writing should be developmentally appropriate, that is, challenging but achievable, with sufficient adult support.

A continuum of reading and writing development is generally accepted and useful for teachers in understanding the goals of literacy instruction and in assessing children's progress toward those goals. Good teachers understand that children do not progress along this developmental continuum in rigid sequence. Rather, each child exhibits a unique pattern and timing in acquiring skills and understanding related to reading and writing.

Like other complex skills, reading and writing are outcomes that result from the continual interplay of development and learning, and therefore a range of individual variation is to be expected in the rate and pace at which children gain literacy skills. Given exposure to appropriate literacy experiences and good teaching during early childhood, most children learn to read at age six or seven, a few learn at four, some learn at five, and others need intensive individualised support to learn to read at eight or nine.

Some children who do not explore books and other print during their early years are likely to need more focused support for literacy development when they enter an educational programme, whether at preschool, kindergarten, or first grade. Other children who enter school speaking little or no English are likely to need instructional strategies in their home language. Given the range within which children typically master reading, even with exposure to print-rich environments and good teaching, a developmentally appropriate expectation is for most children to achieve beginning conventional reading by age seven.

For children with disabilities or special learning needs, achievable but challenging goals for their individual reading and writing development in an inclusive environment are established by teachers, families, and specialists working in collaboration. Early childhood teachers need to understand the developmental continuum of reading and writing and be skilled in a variety of strategies to assess and support individual children's development and learning across the continuum. At the same time teachers must set developmentally appropriate literacy goals for young children and then adapt instructional strategies for children whose learning and development are advanced or lag behind those goals.

Good teachers make instructional decisions based on their knowledge of reading and writing, current research, appropriate expectations, and their knowledge of individual children's strengths and needs. A continuum of reading and writing development is useful for identifying challenging but achievable goals or benchmarks for children's literacy learning, remembering that individual variation is to be expected and supported.

Using a developmental continuum enables teachers to assess individual children's progress against realistic goals and then adapt instruction to ensure that children continue to progress. During the preschool years most children can be expected to function in phase 1 of the developmental continuum, Awareness and Exploration. An appropriate expectation for second grade is Transitional Reading and Writing, while the goal for third grade is Independent and Productive Reading and Writing.

Advanced Reading is the goal for fourth grade and above. As fundamental as the principle of individual variation is the principle that human development and learning occur in and are influenced by social and cultural contexts. Language, reading, and writing are strongly shaped by culture. Children enter early childhood programmes or schools having learned to communicate and make sense of their experiences at home and in their communities.

When the ways of making and communicating meaning are similar at home and in school, children's transitions are eased. However, when the language and culture of the home and school are not congruent, teachers and parents must work together to help children strengthen and preserve their home language and culture while acquiring skills needed to participate in the shared culture of the school.

Most important, teachers must understand how children learn a second language and how this process applies to young children's literacy development. Teachers need to respect the child's home language and culture and use it as a base on which to build and extend children's language and literacy experiences.

Unfortunately teachers too often react negatively to children's linguistic and cultural diversity, equating difference with deficit. Such situations hurt children whose abilities within their own cultural context are not recognised because they do not match the cultural expectations of the school. Failing to recognise children's strengths or capabilities, teachers may underestimate their competence.

Competence is not tied to any particular language, dialect, or culture. Teachers should never use a child's dialect, language, or culture as a basis for making judgments about the child's intellect or capability. Linguistically and culturally diverse children bring multiple perspectives and impressive skills, such as code-switching, to the tasks of learning to speak, read, and write a second language. These self-motivated, self-initiating, constructive thinking processes should be celebrated and used as rich teaching and learning resources for all children.

4

CHILDREN AND LEARN

Learning at school requires students to pay attention, to observe, to memorise, to understand, to set goals and to assume responsibility for their own learning. These cognitive activities are not possible without the active involvement and engagement of the learner. Teachers must help students to become active and goaloriented by building on their natural desire to explore, to understand new things and to master them.

It is a challenge for teachers to create interesting and challenging learning environments that encourage the active involvement of students. The following are some suggestions as to how this can be done:

— Avoid situations where the students are passive listeners for long periods of time.

— Provide students with hands-on activities, such as experiments, observations, projects, etc.

— Encourage participation in classroom discussions and other collaborative activities.

— Organise school visits to museums and technological parks.

— Allow students to take some control over their own learning.

— Taking control over one's learning means allowing students to make some decisions about what to learn and how.

— Assist students in creating learning goals that are consistent with their interests and future aspirations.

SOCIAL ACTIVITIES AND PARTICIPATION

Social participation is the main activity through which learning occurs. Social activity and participation begin early on. Parents interact with their children and through these interactions children acquire the behaviours that enable them to become effective members of society. According to the psychologist Lev Vygotsky, the way children learn is by internalising the activities, habits, vocabulary and ideas of the members of the community in which they grow up. The establishment of a fruitful collaborative and co-operative atmosphere is an essential part of school learning.

Research has shown that social collaboration can boost student achievement, provided that the kinds of interactions that are encouraged contribute to learning. Finally, social activities are interesting in their own right and help to keep students involved in their academic work. Students work harder to improve the quality of their products (essays, projects, artwork, etc.) when they know that they will be shared with other students.

Teachers can do many things to encourage social participation in ways that facilitate learning:

— They can assign students to work in groups and assume the role of a coach/co-ordinator who provides guidance and support to the groups.

— They can create a classroom environment that includes group workspaces where resources are shared.

- Through modelling and coaching, they can teach students how to co-operate with each other.
- They can create circumstances for students to interact with each other, to express their opinions and to evaluate other students' arguments.

An important aspect of social learning is to link the school to the community at large. In this way, students' opportunities for social participation are enlarged.

Many school activities are not meaningful since students understand neither why they are doing them nor what their purpose and usefulness is. Sometimes school activities are not meaningful because they are not culturally appropriate. Many schools are communities where children from diverse cultures learn together. There are systematic cultural differences in practices, in habits, in social roles, etc., that influence learning. Sometimes meaningful activities for students coming from one cultural group are not meaningful to students who are coming from another cultural group.

Teachers can make classroom activities more meaningful by situating them in an authentic context. An example of an authentic context is one in which the activity is typically used in real life. For example, students can improve their oral language and communication skills by participating in debates. They can improve their writing skills by being involved in the preparation of a classroom newspaper. Students can learn science by participating in a community or school environmental project.

The school can be in contact with local scientists and invite them to lecture, or allow the students to visit their laboratories. It is also important for teachers to be aware of the cultural differences of the children in their classroom and to respect these differences. They must see them as strengths to build on, rather than as defects.

Children will feel differently in the classroom if their culture is reflected in the common activities. School routines that are unfamiliar to some children can be introduced gradually so that the transition can be less traumatic for ethnically diverse groups.

NEW INFORMATION TO PRIOR KNOWLEDGE

The idea that people's ability to learn something new follows from what they already know is not new, but more recent research findings have shown that the ability to relate new information to prior knowledge is critical for learning. It is not possible for someone to understand, remember or learn something that is completely unfamiliar. Some prior knowledge is necessary to understand the task at hand. But having the prerequisite prior knowledge is still not sufficient to ensure adequate results.

People must activate their prior knowledge in order to be able to use it for understanding and for learning. Research shows that students do not consistently see the relationships between new material that they read and what they already know. Research also shows that learning is enhanced when teachers pay close attention to the prior knowledge of the learner and use this knowledge as the starting point for instruction. Teachers can help students activate prior knowledge and use it for the task at hand. This can be done in a number of ways.

Teachers can discuss the content of a lesson before starting in order to ensure that the students have the necessary prior knowledge and in order to activate this knowledge. Often students' prior knowledge is incomplete or there are false beliefs and critical misconceptions. Teachers do not simply need to know that students know something about the topic to be introduced. They need to investigate students' prior knowledge in detail so that false beliefs and misconceptions can be identified.

Teachers may need to go back to cover important prerequisite material or ask the students to do some preparatory work on their own. They can ask the kind of question that helps students see relationships between what they are reading and what they already know. Effective teachers can help students to grasp relationships and make connections. They can do so by providing a model or a scaffold that students can use as support in their efforts to improve their performance.

Children develop strategies to help themselves solve problems from an early age. For example, when pre-school children are told to go to the supermarket to buy a list of food items, they often repeat the items on their way to remember them better. These children have discovered rehearsal as a strategy to improve their memory without anybody telling them to do so. When they go to school, children need help from teachers to develop appropriate strategies for solving mathematics problems, when understanding texts, doing science, learning from other students, etc.

When teachers make systematic attempts to teach learning strategies to students substantial gains can result. Strategies are important because they help students understand and solve problems in ways that are appropriate for the situation at hand. Strategies can improve learning and make it faster. Strategies may differ in their accuracy, in their difficulty of execution, in their processing demands and in the range of problems to which they apply. The broader the range of strategies that children can use appropriately, the more successful they can be in problem solving, in reading, in text comprehension and in memorising.

Teachers must recognise the importance of students knowing and using a variety of strategies. The teaching of strategies can be done directly or indirectly. In the latter case, the teacher can give students a task and provide a model of the inquiry process or ask key questions. For example, in reading, teachers can explicitly show students how to outline the important points in a text and how to summarise them. Alternatively, they can ask a group of students to discuss a text and summarise it. They can help in this process by participating in the discussion and by asking critical questions.

In science, teachers can show students how to conduct experiments: how to form hypotheses, how to keep a systematic record of their findings, and how to evaluate them. It is important to ensure that students learn to use these strategies on their own and do not always rely on teachers to provide the necessary support. Teachers need to gradually fade their assistance and allow students to take greater responsibility for their learning.

SELF-REGULATION

The term 'self-regulation' is used here to indicate students' ability to monitor their own learning, to understand when they are making errors, and to know how to correct them. Selfregulation is not the same as being strategic. People can use strategies for learning mechanically without being fully aware of what they are doing. Self-regulation involves the development of specific strategies that help learners evaluate their learning, check their understanding and correct errors when appropriate. Self-regulation requires reflection in the sense of being aware of one's own beliefs and strategies. Reflection can develop through discussion, debates and essays, where children are encouraged to express their opinions and defend them. Another important aspect of reflection is being able to distinguish appearance from reality, common beliefs from scientific knowledge, etc.

Teachers can help students become self-regulated and reflective by providing opportunities:

— To plan how to solve problems, design experiments and read books;

— To evaluate the statements, arguments, solutions to problems of others, as well as of one's self;

— To check their thinking and ask themselves questions about their understanding- (Why am I doing what I am doing? How well am I doing? What remains to be done?);

— To develop realistic knowledge of themselves as learners-(I am good in reading, but need to work on my mathematics);

— To set their own learning goals;

— To know what are the most effective strategies to use and when to use them.

Sometimes existing knowledge can stand in the way of understanding new information. While this is often the case in the learning of science and mathematics, it can apply to all subjectmatter areas. It happens because our current understanding of the physical and social world, of history, of theorising about numbers, etc., is the product of thousands of years of cultural activity that has radically changed intuitive ways of explaining phenomena. For example, in the area of mathematics, many children make mistakes when they use fractions because they use rules that apply to natural numbers only.

Similarly, in the physical sciences, students form various misconceptions. The idea that the Earth is round like a pancake or like a sphere flattened on the top happens because it reconciles the scientific information that the Earth is round, with the intuitive belief that it is flat and that people live upon its top. Such misconceptions do not apply only in young children. They are common in high school and college students as well.

What can teachers do to facilitate the understanding of counterintuitive information?

— Teachers need to be aware that students have prior beliefs and incomplete understandings that can conflict with what is being taught at school.

— It is important to create the circumstances where alternative beliefs and explanations can be externalised and expressed.

— Teachers need to build on the existing ideas of students and slowly lead them to more mature understandings. Ignoring prior beliefs can lead to the formation of misconceptions.

— Students must be provided with observations and experiments that have the potential of showing to them that some of their beliefs can be wrong. Examples from the history of science can be used for this purpose.

— Scientific explanations must be presented with clarity and, when possible, exemplified with models.

— Students must be given enough time to restructure their prior conceptions. In order to do this, it is better to design curricula that deal with fewer topics in greater depth than attempting to cover a great deal of topics in a superficial manner.

All teachers want their students to understand what they are learning and not to memorise facts in a superficial way. Research shows that when information is superficially memorised it is easily forgotten. On the contrary, when something is understood, it is not forgotten easily and it can be transferred to other situations. In order to understand what they are being taught, students must be given the opportunity to think about what they are doing, to talk about it with other students and with teachers, to clarify it and to understand how it applies in many situations.

The following are some tasks teachers can carry out in order to promote understanding of the material that has been taught:

— Ask students to explain a phenomenon or a concept in their own words.

— Show students how to provide examples that illustrate how a principle applies or how a law works.

— Students must be able to solve characteristic problems in the subject-matter area. Problems can increase in difficulty as students acquire greater expertise.

— When students understand the material, they can see similarities and differences, they can compare and contrast, and they can understand and generate analogies.

— Teach students how to abstract general principles from specific cases and generalise from specific examples.

HELPING STUDENTS LEARN

Students often cannot apply what they have learned at school to solve real-world problems. For example, they may learn about Newton's laws at school but fail to see how they apply in real-life situations. Transfer is very important. Why should someone want to go to school if what is learned there does not transfer to other situations and cannot be used outside the school? Teachers can improve students' ability to transfer what they have learned at school by:

— Insisting on mastery of subject matter. Without an adequate degree of understanding, transfer cannot take place.

— Helping students see the transfer implications of the information they have learned.

— Applying what has been learned in one subject-matter area to other areas to which it may be related.

— Showing students how to abstract general principles from concrete examples.

— Helping students learn how to monitor their learning and how to seek and use.

— Teach for understanding rather than for memorisation.

Research shows that people must carry out a great deal of practice to acquire expertise in an area. Even small differences in the amount of time during which people are exposed to information can result in large differences in the information they have acquired. Cognitive psychologists Chase & Simon studied chess experts and found that they had often spent as many as 50,000 hours practising chess.

Research shows that the reading and writing skills of high-school students relate to the hours they have spent on reading and writing. Effective reading and writing requires a lot of practice. Students from dis-advantaged environments who have less opportunities to learn and who miss school because of work or illness will not be expected to do as well at school compared to children who had more time to practice and acquire information.

Many educational programmes are designed to increase one's exposure to learning situations preferably at an early age. Here are some recommendations for teachers that can help students spend more time on learning tasks.

— Increase the amount of time students spend on learning in the classroom.

— Give students learning tasks that are consistent with what they already know.

— Do not try to cover too many topics at once.

— Give students time to understand the new information.

— Help students engage in 'deliberate practice' that includes active thinking and monitoring of their own learning.

— Give students access to books so that they can practice reading at home.

— Be in contact with parents so that they can learn to provide richer educational experiences for their children.

— Children learn best when their individual differences are taken into consideration.

DEVELOPMENTAL AND INDIVIDUAL DIFFERENCES IN LEARNING

Research shows that there are major developmental differences in learning. As children develop, they form new ways of representing the world and they also change the processes and strategies they use to manipulate these representations. In addition, there are important individual differences in learning. Developmental psychologist Howard Gardner has argued that there are many dimensions of human intelligence other than the logical and linguistic skills that are usually valued in most school environments.

Some children are gifted in music, others have exceptional spatial skills (required, for example, by architects and artists), or bodily/kinaesthetic abilities (required by athletes), or abilities to relate to other people, etc. Schools must create the best environment for the development of children taking into consideration such individual differences. The following are recommendations for creating the best environment for the development of children, while recognising their individual differences:

— Learn how to assess children's knowledge, strategies and modes of learning adequately.

— Introduce children to a wide range of materials, activities and learning tasks that include language, mathematics, natural sciences, social sciences, art, music, movement, social understanding, etc.

— Identify students' areas of strength, paying particular attention to the interest, persistence and confidence they demonstrate in different kinds of activities.

— Support students' areas of strength and utilise these areas to improve overall academic performance.

— Guide and challenge students' thinking and learning.

— Ask children thought-provoking questions and give them problems to solve. Urge children to test hypotheses in a variety of ways.

— Create connections to the real world by introducing problems and materials drawn from everyday situations.

— Show children how they can use their unique profiles of intelligence to solve real-world problems.

— Create circumstances for students to interact with people in the community, and particularly with adults who are knowledgeable and enthusiastic about the kinds of things that are of interest to the students.

MOTIVATED LEARNERS

Motivated learners are easy to recognise because they have a passion for achieving their goals and are ready to expend a great deal of effort. They also show considerable determination and persistence. This influences the amount and quality of what is learned. All teachers want to have motivated learners in their classrooms. How can they achieve this? Psychologists distinguish between two kinds of motivation: *extrinsic motivation and intrinsic motivation.*

Extrinsic motivation results when positive rewards are used to increase the frequency of a target behaviour. Praise, high grades, awards, money and food can be used for that effect.

Intrinsic motivation is when learners actively participate in activities without having to be rewarded for it. The child who likes to put together puzzles for the fun of it is intrinsically motivated. An important characteristic of intrinsically motivated learners is their belief that effort is important for success. Teachers can influence students' determination to achieve by their behaviour and the statements they make.

Teachers must use encouraging statements that reflect an honest evaluation of learner performance:

— Recognise student accomplishments.

— Attribute student achievement to internal and not external factors (e.g. 'You have good ideas').

— Help students believe in themselves (e.g. 'You are putting a lot of effort on math and your grades have much improved').

— Provide feedback to children about the strategies they use and instruction as to how to improve them.

— Help learners set realistic goals.

It is also important to:

— Refrain from grouping students according to their ability.

— Ability grouping gives the message that ability is valued more than effort.

— Promote co-operation rather than competition. Research suggests that competitive arrangements that encourage students to work alone to achieve high grades and rewards tend to give the message that what is valued is ability and diminish intrinsic motivation.

— Provide novel and interesting tasks that challenge learners' curiosity and higher-order thinking skills at the appropriate level of difficulty.

5

MORAL EDUCATION

Half a century ago, the question of the optimal age of moral education was purely a matter of believe. Over the past decades so much research has been accumulated that it should be possible to turn this controversy between opposing opinions into a scientific question, and to tell educators how and when it can be nurtured. Moral-psychological research has already helped us to clarify some issues related to moral education.

Almost all children know these values and rules, distinguish them clearly from mere social conventions and personal values, and develop positive attitudes toward them. The transmission of moral values by no means guarantees that children will behave accordingly. It seems that moral attitudes or ideals do not automatically translate into moral behaviour but that moral competencies are required for doing this. In fact, measures of moral judgment competence correlate considerably higher with moral behaviour than moral attitudes do. With regard to the optimal age of moral education, the findings are much less clear. They are even contradictory. While early intervention experiments support the cognitive-developmentalists hypothesis that adolescence is the optimal age for fostering moral competencies, more recent studies seem to refute this hypothesis.

Some textbook authors lean toward the newer findings. They seem to imply that it goes without saying that when two lines of research differ greatly in their findings, the more recent research is more trustworthy. This decision rule would be valid if we can assume

a) that morality is a unitary construct and that both lines of research deal with the same construct and

b) that the differences are merely of methodological nature, that is, that the more recent research is technically superior to the older one.

However, that these two assumptions do not apply in this case and that the older findings are more valid in regard to the question of the optimal age for moral education.

Morality must be described in terms of not just one but of two fundamentally different aspects, namely of an affective aspect and a cognitive aspects. These two aspects can not only be theoretically distinguished but they can also be independently operationalised and measured. On the basis of this dual-aspect-theory, Lind hypothesises that findings will differ depending on the research focus. Research focusing on moral competencies should show that adolescence is the optimal age for fostering the ability to apply moral rules and values to concrete decision-making processes. Research focusing on moral attitudes should reveal that adults sense better the moral expectations of their social environment than youngster do, and adapt their test scores accordingly.

DUAL-ASPECT-THEORY OF MORAL BEHAVIOUR

The dual-aspect-theory of moral behaviour and thinking comprises four postulates, which suggest some important distinctions for discussing the optimal age of moral education. The first two postulates are based on moral philosophy, the two others on empirical research: First, morality must be described in terms of internal states rather than external states, that is, we call a person's behaviour moral only if a person acts upon his or her own moral principles rather than merely complies with external rules or norms. The latter is called rule-conforming behaviour.

Furthermore, the description of a person's morality must involve both always both affective and cognitive aspects. In other words, the moral goodness of our behaviour depends both on the moral ideals or principles to which we aspire and on our ability to judge and act accordingly. The affective aspect of moral judgment behaviour is defined as the moral ideals, values and attitudes a person holds. More specifically, it is defined as the moral perspective that marks the horizon of his or her subjective moral universe.

Kohlberg's six stages of moral perspective-taking provide an appropriate scheme for typifying the affective aspect of subjects' moral thought and behaviour. Moral judgment competence, the cognitive aspect of moral judgment behaviour, develops through four the phases that Piaget described:

- *Amorality or anomia*: The child lacks moral sensibility and does not care about right and wrong; he or she pays no attention at all to moral perspectives;
- *Imitation*: The child merely mimics moral language but sees no implications for his or her behaviour;
- *Heteronomy*: The child subordinates his or her behaviour to moral perspectives but without a clear understanding of their meaning; the child usually acts in a rigid, all-or-nothing way because he or she makes decisions under only one moral perspective but is not able to integrate different moral

perspectives and make judgments in a differentiated way; he or she relies mostly on external authorities;

— *Autonomy*: The child is able to integrate many moral perspectives and make an integrated and differentiated moral judgment that does justice both to the abstract principles and the concrete situation involved. Moral autonomy is not absolute but always in regard to a particular moral perspective. That is, a child is call morally autonomous in regard to a particular level of moral perspective-taking; he or she considers all moral perspectives available to him or her on that stage for making a decision, even though they may conflict with his or her most salient one.

Second, while we can clearly distinguish both aspects of morality and, therefore, can describe and measure both the cognitive and the affective aspect in a logically independent way (the degree of moral judgment competence needs not be linked with particular moral principles), both aspects are not separable, that is, they cannot be conceived of as being two different substances, components or sets of behaviour. Hence, we must measure a person's moral attitudes and competencies with one and the same measuring instrument, but must not confuse both aspects.

Third, the dual-aspect-theory implies that development of both aspects is time-lagged parallel. "Time-lagged" means that is the acquisition of certain moral perspective or orientations will precede the development of the cognitive competencies needed for autonomous moral action. In other words, moral perspectives serve as goals or ideals for the development of the moral competencies needed to approximate them in everyday-action. "Parallel" means that, while both aspects can be logically distinguished and independently measured, they will correlate empirically. That is, the greater a child's moral judgment competence the more he or she will prefer higher over lower moral perspectives, whereas "higher" and "lower" refers here to Kohlberg's Stage model.

Fourth, the dual-aspect-theory suggests that both aspects of moral behaviour and development require distinct methods for their change or enhancement. While methods of direct teaching or transmittance of moral values seems to be well suited for changing children's moral attitudes, they do not seem appropriate for enhancing the development of moral competencies. Teaching methods, which require children to solve concrete behavioural problems, seem more appropriate. Such teaching methods have been suggested by Kohlberg and his colleagues, e.g., the Moral Dilemma Discussion (MDD) method.

The MDD method works similar to medical immunisation. Whereas medical treatment stimulates the body's immune system by introducing a mildly toxic dose of a virus, the MDD method confronts the child's cognitive system with moral dilemmas that are semi-real, that is, dilemmas which are real enough to arouse a child's moral emotions but are not so real as to have real consequences for the child. This theory postulates that the cognitive and the affective aspect of moral behaviour are parallel. In contrast to both these theorists, we believe that these two aspects cannot only be theoretically distinguished but can also be measured independently from each other. Like Piaget we also believe that the affective and the cognitive side of human behaviour cannot, and should not, be viewed as separate components but as distinguishable aspects or properties of behaviour.

Lind's Moral Judgment Test (MJT) is proof that it is possible, to measure the two aspects of moral judgment behaviour independently, without separating them into different components or test items. Through this achievement, now we can evaluate the effects of moral education programmes on the competence aspect of moral judgment without confusing them with the effects on moral affects or attitudes. Given these clarifications, we assume that, if taught and measured appropriately, moral education should show its greatest effects during adolescence when children develop their capacity of abstract reasoning.

The optimal age for applying the MDD method is the age between 10 and 16 years of age. Drawing upon Piaget's theory of cognitive development, they argue that "pre-adolescence is a favored or 'critical' period for intervention into moral development". Therefore, if adolescents do not receive educational aid, some "might be expected to stabilise at the preconventional level, as do most adolescent delinquents". "With the adolescent only beginning to acquire formal operational capacities," Enright et al. noted, "during this period, a programme designed to induce new cognitive acquisitions could be expected maximally effective". Thus, there should be no, or only spurious, effect of moral teaching if teaching is aimed at changing moral values or if the measurement taps largely the affective rather than the cognitive aspect of moral judgment behaviour.

Recently, these two conditions of effective moral education have been questioned by Rest and his associates. They conclude a) that non-developmental methods of direct teaching have greater effects than cognitive-developmental methods and b) that adulthood, not adolescence, is the optimal age of education. A growing number of textbook authors accept this conclusion as state of the art. Young adults have a larger capacity to examine moral dilemmas from a personal standpoint. Astonishingly, this assertion is accepted without discussing the fact that it fundamentally contradicts cognitive-developmental theory and most earlier research findings

The high correlation so often been found between both aspects vanishes in educational settings because the distinctive features of competencies and attitudes become highly salient. Subjects attitude scores can change in any direction within a very short time, either because their attitudes really change or because the subjects have reasons to simulate such change. In contrast, subjects can acquires competencies, skills, abilities and alike only slowly (as it takes much exercise to develop them) and they will lose them also slowly rather than abruptly. Experimentally, competencies and attitudes can be clearly distinguished when we instruct people to simulate them "upward".

While people should be able to exhibit any attitude that we instruct them to simulate, they should not be able to simulate only a lower, not a higher, level of moral competency than they actually possess. Thus, while intervention aiming at a change of students' moral values might show impressive changes due to students desire to please their teacher, such interventions should show no increase in students' moral competencies. Therefore, from the dual-aspect point of view, we hypothesise that the vast differences in findings concerning the optimal age of moral education can be mostly accounted for by the confounding of moral attitudes and moral competencies in the measurement of moral development.

If the aim of moral education is the enhancement of moral competencies and if these are taught with appropriate methods like the MDD method, then the optimal age for it should be adolescence. In contrast, if the teacher wants, for some reason, for students to get high scores on moral attitudes scales and he or she makes sure that the students know what they are expected to say, then higher-age-groups might produce better results. Adults might be more "able" to acquiesce than adolescents, who might have difficulties to discern what attitudes their teachers expect from them.

Intervention studies based on Kohlberg's MJI appear to give the most accurate and defendable picture of educational effects as the MJI is widely regarded as the best "cognitive" measure of moral development. Yet MJT-based studies leave also some questions open because the MJI is not a pure competence measure but confounds to some extend moral attitudes and competencies (a subject must simultaneously have a high judgment competence and also prefer Stage-6-Morality to get a high score on the MJI) and it has not yet been thoroughly tested for fakability. These open questions can be answered by MJT-based studies because the MJT has been designed to measure moral attitudes and moral competence simultaneously without confouding them, and which has withstood rigorous faking experiments.

In agreement with expert's judgment, we will report here figures of practical significance or effect size but not of statistical significance. For many decades statisticians are castigating the use of significance tests for being mostly out of place and as impeding rather than aiding the progress of educational science.

MJI-based Findings

Pre-adolescence is the optimal age: Blatt and Kohlberg, who used the Moral Judgment Interview for evaluating effects, give us the first experimental data on the validity of the cognitive-developmental hypothesis regarding the optimal age for using the Moral Dilemma Discussion method. In their first study of 11 to 12-year-old students, they found that the MDD method was highly effective. These pre-adolescents gained on average 66 MMS points, that is, more than a half stage, on a scale from 100 to 600 (Stage 6), whereas the control group showed no gains. They also found that this effect was still discernible after one year when they followed up their subjects. After one year, the children's MMS scores dropped a little, but only 11 points. This contrasts with the changes in a control group, which showed hardly any gains (only four points), but a drop of scores in the follow-up assessment.

In their second study, Blatt and Kohlberg found that older children, ages 15 to 16, also gained markedly (36 MMS points). In their follow-up assessment one year after the intervention experiment, they found a further increase of approximately 30 points. So the gross increase for this older group was also more than 60 points.

The MJI-based studies clearly support the assumption that the optimal age for the MDD method is adolescence and not adulthood. Although, the MDD method has also a developmental effect in younger and in older age-groups, the adolescents aging from 11 to 16 gain most.

DIT-based Findings

Adulthood is the Optimal Age: In contrast to these findings, intervention studies evaluated with Rest's Defining Issues Test come to a quite different conclusion. Test come to a quite different conclusion. To make the findings in these studies better comparable with the Kohlbergian studies, the d-indices, reported by Rest and Thomas are converted here into correlation coefficients. When comparing these findings with MJI-based studies, two findings are most noteworthy. First, in DIT-based studies, adults gain considerably from moral cognitive interventions. Second, in DIT-based studies, the MDD method seems to produce hardly any effects in adolescents and young adults.

Rest and his colleagues suggest three possible explanations for the age differences in effect sizes. First, they hypothesise that because adult subjects usually volunteered rather than were assigned to the moral education programme, they may show a greater willingness to participate in it. However, this explanation does not account for the fact that this phenomenon appeared only in DIT-based intervention studies but not in MJI-based studies.

Second, they argued that interventions with adults might be more powerful because adults can draw on more experiences. Again, this argument cannot account for the fact that in MJI-based studies adults gained less than adolescents. Moreover, this argument works both ways: we may also expect that adults gain less from MDD method because, as Kohlberg would argue, this method foremost stimulates competencies that the highly developed subjects already have.

Third, they suggest that the DIT might be relatively insensitive effects of the MDD and other methods of moral education in adolescents. Indeed, the P index used with the DIT for measuring moral development, is designed to measure only an increase of preferences for stage five and six reasoning, but not shifts within lower stage reasoning. "The P score indicates," as Rest point out, "the extent to which the subject considers the <Principled' items as most important. One way to interpret the DIT's P score is the extent to which the subject makes moral judgements like a moral philosopher".

Besides the explanations which the authors considered, there is still another methodological explanation for the overall low effect-sizes. The DIT was developed on the basis of classical test theory, which suggests item selection procedures to maximise both

(a) inter-individual variation and (b) individual stability of scores, to get a high "reliability" coefficient for the test. This strategy of test construction partly undermines the purpose of developmental and educational research, namely to measure change as an consequence of educational efforts. Making a test highly stable or "reliable" is good for the purpose of sorting and selecting people but not for the aims usually pursued in education. Thus, the lack of effects shown by adolescent samples may be indeed a methodological artifact.

The DIT shows the MDD to be effective in adults only **(a) because it may reflect mostly, if not exclusively changes in moral attitudes and, therefore, be susceptible to the so-called "Hawthorne-effect" and (b) because it is insensitive to changes in the range of moral-cognitive development for which the MDD method is designed.** This could mean, by the intervention programme, the adult subjects might not become more competent to make moral judgments but might try to please the moral expectations of their teachers who want them to make moral judgments like a moral philosopher. With adolescents, either the DIT is not sensitive enough to show such effects, or adolescents are less inclined to acquiesce.

Several lines of evidence support this hypothesis. In an experimental study subjects can simulate or fake DIT-scores upward. In DIT-based studies, direct teaching methods, like exposing the subjects to Kohlberg's stage theory, produce much higher effect size than the MDD method. Finally, Penn shows that the "direct teaching of fundamentals," that is, the indoctrination of moral values, has a stronger effect on P-score gains (d = .65, r = .31) than the moral dilemma discussion method.

All these studies have no bearing on Kohlberg's claim that the MDD method can effectively simulate moral judgment competence, because these effects have not been measured with tests of moral competence. In studies using the Kohlberg interview method, direct teaching methods hardly showed any effects and they were less persistent than the effects of the MDD method. So the empirical ground is still scarce for making a judgment on Schläfli et al.'s hypothesis that, to profit from the MDD method, a higher level of moral judgment competence is necessary than adolescents usually possess.

The contention that the MDD method has substantial effects only in adulthood seems to be based on a methodological artifact. It is supported only by intervention studies using Rest's Defining Issues Test. The DIT is hardly sensitive to changes on lower level of moral reasoning as are typically found in adolescents, the main addressees of the MDD method. The positive effects of the MDD method in adult samples can be explained through the fact that the DIT is prone to the Hawthorne-effect because, like most attitude measures, it can be faked upward. The adults subjects may readily guess the intentions of the experimenter and respond to the DIT in a way that please him or her. This explanation is reinforced by the fact that, in adult samples, direct methods of value teaching have a greater effect size than cognitive methods like the MDD method.

The differential findings of studies using measures of moral competence versus measures moral attitudes, and using cognitive-developmental versus direct moral teaching methods, reinforce the distinctions made in Lind's dual-aspect-theory. The effects of moral education differ greatly depending on which aspect we address in a moral education programme and which aspects we actually measure. If these distinctions are not made, the findings may look confusing, if not contradictory. In respect to moral education, this finding adds to a bulk of literature that shows that the Moral Dilemma Discussion method is a powerful method for fostering moral development in adolescents.

In contrast, methods like value indoctrination and moral behaviour drills have shown to be little effective in fostering moral development. If new improved variants of these methods are suggested, they should be submitted to the same kind of rigorous empirical testing as the MDD method has been. One caveat is in turn. We can also speculate that the MDD method affects not only the level of moral judgment competence but other competencies and motivations, and, therefore, MDD methods are also beneficial for adults and for children prior to their adolescence. Research on those speculations are still scarce. But studies reviewed here and my extensive experiences with moral dilemma discussion in kindergarten, college, university and adult groups, suggests that they may be correct.

Through the MDD method, developmentally advance subjects seem to gain new insights into the "actual" meaning of moral values and explore a wide range of action-consequences of otherwise abstract moral principles. And, they also learn to appreciate the MDD method as an effective method for moral learning and dilemma solution. In the long run, this insight may foster the ability of self-sustaining moral development. People may look up or construct MDD situations for themselves without the help of teachers and educators.

6

STUDENT-CENTRED LEARNING

The term Student-Centred Learning (SCL) is widely used in the teaching and learning literature. Many terms have been linkedwith student-centred learning, such as flexible learning, experiential learning, self-directed learning and therefore the slightly overused term 'student-centred learning' can mean different things to different people. In addition, in practice it is also described by a range of terms and this has led to confusion surrounding its implementation.

The concept of student-centred learning has been credited as early as 1905 to Hayward and in 1956 to Dewey's work. Carl Rogers, the father of client-centred counselling, is associated with expanding this approach into a general theory of education. The term student-centred learning was also associated with the work of Piaget and more recently with Malcolm Knowles. Rogers, in his book 'Freedom to Learn for the 80s', describes the shift in power from the expert teacher to the student learner, driven by a need for a change in the traditional environment where in this 'so-called educational atmosphere, students become passive, apathetic and bored'.

In the School system, the concept of child-centred education has been derived, in particular, from the work of Froebel and the idea that the teacher should not 'interfere with this process of maturation, but act as a guide'. Simon highlighted that this was linked with the process of development or 'readiness', i.e. the child will learn when he/she is ready.

The paradigm shift away from teaching to an emphasis on learning has encouraged power to bemoved fromthe teacher to the student. The teacher-focused/ transmission of information formats, such as lecturing, have begun to be increasingly criticised and this has paved the way for a widespread growth of 'student-centred learning' as an alternative approach. However, despite-wide-spread use of the term, one of the issues with student-centred learning is the fact that 'many institutions or educators claim to be putting student-centred learning into practice, but in reality they are not'.

TWO BROAD ORIENTATIONS IN TEACHING

The teacher centred/content oriented conception and the student centred/learning oriented conceptions. In a very useful breakdown of these orientations he supports many other authors views in relation to student-centred view including: that knowledge is constructed by students and that the lecturer is a facilitator of learning rather than a presenter of information.

The important pre-condition for student-centred learning as the need for a leader or person who is perceived as an authority figure in the situation, is sufficiently secure within herself (himself) and in her (his) relationship to others that she (he) experiences an essential trust in the capacity of others to think for themselves, to learn for themselves.

Choice in the area of the learning is emphasised by Burnard, as he interprets Rogers' ideas of student-centredness as 'students might not only choose what to study, but how and why that topic might be an interesting one to study'. He also emphasises Rogers' belief that students' perceptions of the world were important, that they were relevant and appropriate. This definition therefore emphasises the concept of students having 'choice' in their learning.

Teacher-centred learning strategies as the focus on the teacher transmitting knowledge, fromthe expert to the novice. In contrast, they describe student-centred learning as focusing on the students' learning and 'what students do to achieve this, rather than what the teacher does'. This definition emphasises the concept of the student 'doing'. Articulate broader, more comprehensive definitions. Some of the literature on student-centred learning to include the followings tenets:

— 'The reliance on active rather than passive learning,
— An emphasis on deep learning and understanding,
— Increased responsibility and accountability on the part of the student,
— An increased sense of autonomy in the learner
— An interdependence between teacher and learner,
— Mutual respect within the learner teacher relationship,
— And a reflexive approach to the teaching and learning process on the part of both teacher and learner.'

Student-centred courses as those that emphasise: learner activity rather than passivity; students' experience on the course outside the institution and prior to the course; process and competence, rather than content; where the key decisions about learning aremade by the student through negotiation with the teacher. What is to be learnt, how and when it is to be learnt, with what outcome, what criteria and standards are to be used, how the judgements are made and by whom these judgements are made. Use in second level education (post-primary), entitled 'A Guide to Student-Centred Learning', they present the main principles of student-centred learning as:

— The learner has full responsibility for her/his learning.

— Involvement and participation are necessary for learning.

— The relationship between learners is more equal, promoting growth, development.

— The teacher becomes a facilitator and resource person.

The theoretical standing of student-centred learning is often surprisingly absent in the literature. However, it appears to relate primarily to the constructivist view of learning in the importance it places on activity, discovery and independent learning.

Cognitive theory also highlights activity but in a different form than that supported by the constructivists. The cognitive view supports the idea that the activity of learning is computed in the head, or as often described 'in the mind'. The constructivist view of activity is related more to performing physical activities, for example, projects; practicals.

Student-centred learning has some connections with the social constructivist view, which emphasises activity and the importance of communities of practice/others in the learning process. However, the definitions of SCL do not necessarily highlight the importance of peers in learning.

Implementation of Student-centred Learning

Learning is often presented in this dualism of either

student-centred learning or teacher-centred learning. In the reality of practice the situation is less black and white. Amore useful presentation of student-centred learning is to see these terms as either end of a continuum, using the three concepts regularly used to describe student-centred learning.

Teacher-centred learning	**Student-centred learning**
Low level of student choice	High level of student choice
Student passive	Student active
Power is primarily with teacher	Power is primarily with student
◄	►

Figure 1: Student-centred and teacher-centred continuum

In examining how you might look at this in practice, it is worth thinking how far up the continuum you are able to move within the contextual barriers in your teaching situation.

Curriculum Design

In relation to curriculum design, student-centredness includes the idea that students have choice in what to study, how to study. Modularisation, which will be expected in all European undergraduate courses by 2006, provides a structure that allows students an element of choice in what modules they study. Choice in the curriculum is not without its difficulties and Edwards argues about the dangers of individuality in the concept of the social learner and how this can in a seemingly contradictory way lead to dis-empowerment.

One student-centred approach to curriculum design, Problem-Based Learning (PBL), allows for some choice within a programme of areas that students may study. It allows students to set some of their own learning objectives/outcomes, dependent on prior knowledge.

Problem-Based Learning, through the use of problems/ issues/triggers, encourages the students to develop their own learning goals, thereby filling in the gaps in their knowledge or understanding.

Table 1: Learning Outcomes and Student-centred Learning

Student–centred learning Outcomes: Some examples	***Traditional Learning Outcomes/ Objectives***
By the end of this modules: you (the student) will be able to:	*The course will cover:*
Recognise structure of heart	The anatomy of the heart
Critique one of Yeats' poems	A selection of Yeats poems

This element of choice or control is referred to in many of the definitions of student-centred learning. Student-centred learning involves 'increased responsibility and accountability on the part of the student'. Problem-based learning is higher up the student choice aspect of the SCL continuum in figure1, than the usual problem-solving or problem-oriented exercises performed in a lecture/ tutorial. These approaches are more controlled by the teacher in their presentation and outcome.

However, they are useful in addressing the active learning aspect of student-centred learning. Other approaches to curriculum design also support the idea of student choice and activity in learning, for example, the systems-based approach, resource-based learning, and experiential/ personal relevance approach.

A growing practice in course design internationally is the writing of learning outcomes/objectives focusing on what the student will be able to do, rather than on the content being covered by the teacher. This practice is an example of the move towards student-centred learning in the curriculum and helps to shift the emphasis on the learner as opposed to a coverage model by the teacher.

Re-iterate the importance of this shift in emphasis. Table 1 presents some examples of student-centred learning outcomes.

TEACHING/LEARNING METHODS

The first strategy was to make the student more active in acquiring knowledge and skills and might include exercises in class, use of CAL (computer assisted learning) packages etc.

The second strategy was to make the student more aware of what they are doing and why they are doing it.

A third strategy is a focus on interaction, such as the use of tutorials and other discussion groups.

The final strategy is the focus on transferable skills. This last strategy is not mentioned in other definitions of the student-centred learning but does look beyond the immediate course requirements to other benefits to the student in later employment.

Table 2: Student-centred learning/teaching methods

Outside of the lecture format	In the Lecture
Independent projects	Buzz groups (short discussion in twos)
Group discussion	Pyramids/snowballing (Buzz groups continuing the discussion into larger groups)
Peer mentoring of other students	Cross-overs (mixing students into groups by letter/number allocations)
Debates	Rounds (giving turns to individual students to talk)
Field-trips	Quizes
Practicals	Writing reflections on learning (3/4 minutes)
Reflective diaries, learning journals	Student class presentations
Computer assisted learning	Role play
Choice in subjects for study/projects	Poster presentations

Writing newspaper article	Students producing mind maps in class
Portfolio development	

Table 2 highlights a sample of student-centred learning/ teaching methods and includes some ideas for lecturers both within (more teacher-centred) and outside of the lecture format. You may consider, however, in striving to reduce the amount of lecture contact hours for more student-centred formats, where possible.

ASSESSMENT PRACTICES

Some of the difficulties highlighted in the literature in the area of assessment, for example,

a) That the giving ofmarks and grades are over emphasised,while the giving of advice and the learning function are under emphasised,

b) Pupils are compared with one another which highlights competition rather than personal improvement. He also explains the concept of self-assessment as essential activity to help students 'take responsibility for their own learning', an important aspect of SCL.

Foucault argued that the examination was a technique of power, where a student is 'controlled through a system 'micro-penalties', the constant giving of marks which constitutes a whole field of surveillance'. The use of the written examination is still a strong practice in today's Universities and is primarily a summative assessment, i.e. an assessment for judgement or accreditation. The addition of more formative assessment, which emphasises feedback to students on their learning, would 'enhance their (student) learning'. By developing more formative assessment in your courses you can provide a focus for the student by highlighting their learning gaps and areas that they can develop.

Examples of formative assessment include feedback on essays, written comments on assignments, grades during the year that do not add to end of year mark and multiple-choice questions/answers for feedback only. The addition of more formative assessment encourages a more student-centred approach. Table 3 presents practical examples of student-centred assessments. Further details of some of these assessments can be seen on the UCD Centre for Teaching and Learning website.

Table 3: Student–centred assessments

• Diaries, logs and journals	• Projects
• Portfolios	• Group work
• Peer/self assessment	• Profiles
• Learning contracts and negotiated assessment	• Skills and competencies

Peer and self-assessment both give some control and responsibility back to the student, emphasising 'an increased sense of autonomy in the learner'. Learning contracts/negotiated contracts are goals set by the student, depending on their learning gaps, which are in turn negotiated with the lecturer. The contract can also highlight the manner in which the student would like to be assessed in order to demonstrate that they have reached the goals.

Table 4: Assessment process and student-centred learning

Involving students at the stage when the task is set:	• Choosing the assessment task • Setting the assessment task • Discussion the assessment criteria • Setting the assessment criteria
Involving students at the stage after the task is completed:	• Making self-assessment comments • Making peer-assessment feedback comments

- Suggesting self-assessment grades/marks
- Negotiating self-assessment grades/marks
- Assigning self-assessment grades/marks
- Assigning peer-assessment grades/marks

This can add choice in what to study and, in addition, choice in how the student will be assessed. Choice is one of the key terms in relation to student-centred learning. The concept of negotiation of learning also addresses the unique change in relationship between lecturer and student. The suggestions in Table 4 abovemay seema large jump fromyour current practices, therefore, you might consider moving your assessment practice slightly up the teacher/student-centred continuum. An example of a small but significant change is to provide a choice of essay topics and exam questions as a manageable starting point.

CRITIQUES OF STUDENT-CENTRED LEARNING

The use of student-centred learning appears to be reflective of today's society where choice and democracy are important concepts. Several studies on student-centred learning and found that overall it was an effective approach. A six-year study in Helsinki, which compared traditional and activating instruction, found that the activating group developed better study skills and understanding, but were slower in their study initially. Equally, Hall and Saunders found that students had increased participation, motivation and grades in a first year information technology course.

In addition, 94% of the students would recommend it to others over the more conventional approach. Student-centred learning, despite its popularity, is not without its critics. The main critique of student-centred learning is its focus on the individual learner. In addition, there are some difficulties in its implementation, i.e. the resources needed to implement it, the belief system of the students and staff, and students' lack of familiarity with the term.

Student-centred learning, in the School system, can be in danger of focusing completely on the individual learner and taken to its extreme does not take into account the needs of the whole class. Simon highlights the point that 'if each child is unique, and each requires a specific pedagogical approach appropriate to him or her and to no other, the construction of an all embracing pedagogy or general principles of teaching become an impossibility'.

The dangers associated with student-centredness in adult education where in empowering an individual there is a potential danger of 'a person's physical isolation from other learners'. The importance of the social context of learning and the value of interaction with peers is emphasised in the socio-cultural view of learning.

The concept of being an independent learner choosing his/her own route of learning, may in fact drive some of the sociability out of the learning process if care is not taken to emphasise the importance of peers. In relation to this individuality, Lea et al.'s study on psychology students highlighted their concern over being abandoned or isolated from other supports in a student-centred learning approach.

Student-centred learning as a Western approach to learning and may not necessarily transfer to the developing countries, such asNamibia, where there are limited resources and different learning cultures. It can be equally hard at times to see how the approach can be economical in the large classes associated with many current University undergraduate courses. Student-centred learning (SCL) was more prevalent in the later years of the student degrees, and this they believe is often down to class sizes.

Another concern regarding student centred learning is the belief that students hold in relation to their learning. Students who value or have experienced more teacher-focused approaches, may reject the student-centred approach as frightening or indeed not within their remit. Prosser and Trigwell's work in higher education emphasises the different belief systems held by staff and students. They found that lecturers with a teacher-centred approach to teaching held views that students should accommodate information rather than developing and changing their conceptions and understanding.

The reverse was true for those with more student-centred approaches to their teaching. Students can change their view on learning and as they move through the years so to may their views on student-centred learning change. Finally, students' familiarity with the term can be poor. A study on 48 psychology students in the University of Plymouth on students' attitudes to student-centred learning. They found that, despite a University student-centred policy, 60% of the students had not heard of the term.

7

COLLABORATIVE LEARNING TOOLS

Three models of mind that could guide our conceptions of learning and cognition: **mind as computer** (a symbol manipulation device), **mind as brain** (a parallel distributed processing device), and mind as rhizome (an infinity of connections with and within the social cultural milieu). Each of these metaphors points to a view of instruction in general and of collaborative learning tools in particular:

— *Learning as information processing*—a cognitive skills approach.

— *Learning as experiential growth and pattern recognition*—a cognitive constructivist approach.

— *Learning as a socio-cultural dialogic activity*—a social constructivist or socio-cultural approach. If learning is predominantly information processing, then instruction should provide for efficient communication of information and effective strategies for remembering.

If learning is pre-dominantly experiential growth, then instruction should focus on experiences and activities that promote the individual development of the appropriate cognitive networks or mind maps. And, finally, if learning is pre-dominantly a socio-cultural dialogic, then instruction should provide opportunities for embedding learning in authentic tasks leading to participation in a community of practice.

But each of these views presumes the availability, in the world of experience, of tools and structures to support them. In a way, each of these three views can be identified and embodied in the tools and cultural practices of the late 20th century; though none is so apparent and consequential as the socio-cultural. Recent developments in cultural tools and instructional practices have allowed rapid advances in socio-cultural theory by providing embodiments and instantiations of this theory undreamed of only decades ago.

Daily advances in fiber optics, multimedia, and telecomputing technology continue to force new sectors of society to grapple with information access, transmission, and collaboration issues. In the midst of this social and technological drama, vast resources at our fingertips are restructuring the way we humans work, live, learn, and generally interact regardless of "geography, distance, resources, or disability".

Technology is becoming increasingly interactive and distributed, such that individual learners have available, at rapidly declining cost, the means to participate in incredibly complex networks of information, resources, and instruction. For instance, Internet navigation and discovery tools like the World Wide Web (WWW) have brought to many of our desktops an immense array of text, video, sound, and communication resources unthinkable even 10 years ago.

Such changes cannot fail to influence our views of the teaching-learning process and the education of our children. During the past few years we have all witnessed the exploding interest in the Internet among teachers, students, and other learning communities. But the underlying views of learning held by students and teachers of the Internet remain unclear.

With the dramatic growth in both the means and impact of collaborative communication, there is a heightened need for theoretically based collaborative educational learning tool use. At the same time, educational leaders need re-assurance and guidance that as the formats for electronic collaboration proliferate, computer-mediated communication will enhance student-teacher and student-student interaction and positively reorganise the learning process of K-12 schools and institutions of higher learning.

Some educators claim that online environments are particularly appropriate for collaborative learning approaches because they emphasise group interaction. But as the menu of technology choices in schools, workplaces, and on college campuses escalates, instructional decisions regarding how to communicate with learners across these settings are becoming increasingly critical and complex.

The lack of pedagogical guidance about integrating tools for collaboration and communication into one's classroom or training setting leaves instructors across educational settings with mounting dilemmas and confusion. Predictably, the traditional teacher-centred model in which knowledge is "transmitted" from teacher to learner is rapidly being replaced by alternative models of instruction (e.g., learner-centred, constructivist, and sociocultural ideas) in which the emphasis is on guiding and supporting students as they learn to construct their understanding of the culture and communities of which they are a part.

In the process of shifting our attention to the constructive activity of the learner, here recognise the need to anchor learning in real-world or authentic contexts that make learning meaningful and purposeful. The blending of these technological and pedagogical advancements has elevated the importance of research on electronic student dialogue, text conferencing, information sharing, and other forms of collaboration. Clearly, as specialised software is developed to support the exchange of information across workstations and various instructional strategies are experimented with and modified, collaborative tools will present unique opportunities for facilitating, augmenting, and redefining learning environments.

Rapid tool development during the 1990s has naturally multiplied concerns within a number of human-computer interaction subfields for identifying, empirically examining, and adapting the design of collaborative learning tools. In fact, one such sub-field, computer-supported collaborative learning (CSCL), has merged various technological and instructional trends to offer major promise for coping with this current change.

Advances in interactive technologies for learning collaboration within CSCL are evident in new journals, conferences, technology tool announcements, instructional labs, and professional organisations. Prominent CSCL technologies for computer conferencing and collaboration are bringing students close to real-world environments and mentoring situations. As these collaborative technologies provide increasing opportunities for working with online communities of learners, the pedagogic potential of every connected classroom multiplies.

Given all these new technologies for conferencing and collaboration, faculty in higher education as well as those in public schools and the corporate world have a growing number of instructional possibilities to consider. And there is certainly no sign of a letup in collaborative tool development. The primary issue facing these educators, therefore, is what sort of framework they will have for incorporating these tools for learning collaboration into K-12, higher education, and corporate classrooms.

LEARNER-CENTRED PRINCIPLES (LCPS)

In 1990, the American Psychological Association (APA) and the Mid-continent Regional Educational Laboratory (McREL) joined forces to create a task force on psychology in education that recognised that research and theory on learning, development, and motivation was not having as great an impact in school reform and restructuring activities as expected. As a result, an eclectic mix of 12 learner-centred principles (LCPs) were drafted, which later evolved into 14 basic principles from the APA.

Because these learner-centred principles have extensive research backing, they have begun to provide a foundation for educational reform and transformation across age levels and organisations. With all the media attention on tangible and costeffective changes in schools, these reform efforts, not surprisingly, are especially conspicuous in technology-rich learning environments wherein the role of the teacher is under intense scrutiny and transformation.

Technology-enhanced instructional settings, such as distance learning, offer special opportunities for implementing learner-centred principles and demonstrating them in action. They pointed out that distance-learning technology can offer greater opportunity to experience learning activities that are internally driven and constructed, goal oriented and reflective, personally meaningful and authentic, collaborative and socially negotiated, and adaptive to individual needs and cultural backgrounds.

Such construction of knowledge and emphasis on mental operations also aligns with the third, fourth, and fifth LCPs. More strikingly, the sixth LCP, on the "context of learning," explicitly notes that learning is influenced by environmental factors such as technology, instruction, and culture.

The three motivationally related LCPs point to the role of novelty, optimal difficulty, curiosity, personal choice, control, effort, and emotions. Certainly these, too, have applicability in technology-mediated settings. The intrigue of answering questions posted by one's foreign peers as well as the delight of posting one's ideas and work on the WWW builds a personal sense of pride and ownership over the task. The linkage between collaborative technologies and learner-centred instruction, therefore, is extremely strong with both the cognitive and motivational principles.

The third category of LCPs relates to developmental and social factors in learning. Adapting collaborative technology to the developmental issues stated in the 10th LCP is simultaneously the most tenuous and promising of these principles, however. Technology alone is not adaptive, but the design and use of it most definitely can be. This LCP clearly corresponds to the supposed benefits of electronic conferencing and collaboration tools. It is here, in the social relations, that the cognitive and motivational activities addressed by the first 9 LCPs spring forth. The social interactional nature of collaborative educational technologies can foster many emotions and cognitions, including:

— The tension of debate with students from distant lands who may come within one's field of vision,

— The query of a student seeking to fill in a gap in his or her knowledge base,

— The warming feedback of a keyboard-generated smile, and

— The encouragement of someone recently befriended on the electronic superhighway. In effect, a common ground of interest and understanding is becoming a more determinant factor of who one communicates with than some shared "physical" space or geographic proximity.

The fortunes of the learner-centred movement may, in fact, hinge on the success of emerging collaborative technologies in promoting interaction among those with common interests as well as finding learners new proximities of interest along the way.

Finally, the last three LCPs, related to individual differences in learning such as prior knowledge, linguistic and cultural backgrounds, and challenging standards, each can be linked to collaborative learning technologies. The use of global communication tools can make learner differences in prior knowledge more salient, while forcing learners to consider variations between the way they view the world and those individuals from distinctly different social, economic, cultural, and linguistic backgrounds.

At the same time, when students gather information to share with classmates from other cultures, their performance becomes elevated as one does not want to "look dumb" to his or her foreign peers. In this way, perhaps more challenging learning standards are established for both parties as is hoped for in the final LCP. These 14 LCPs have arisen, in part, to satisfy public school teachers and higher education faculty who are no longer satisfied teaching in the familiar and routine way in which they themselves were taught. Many of these educators are seeking to use collaborative technologies to build new interaction patterns and learning communities based on a philosophy that puts the learner first.

But although the emergence of more learner-centred teaching practices and technology tools for constructing knowledge applies to a myriad of school settings, most teachers still lack the support and direction to use collaborative technology from such a learner-centred perspective. For instance, teachers previously trained in the benefits of collaborative learning need to know how to embed grouping strategies when using CSCL tools. Furthermore, teachers trained in teacher-centred technologies such as overheads and videotape, or tool-centred media such as computer-assisted instruction or databases and spreadsheets, are now being asked to adopt CSCL technologies that place increasing responsibility for learning squarely in the hands of the learner.

Fourteen individual statements are helpful but not enough. Teachers need assistance in identifying opportunities for the use of these principles in instruction and in evaluating their effectiveness. CSCL tools should provide a number of windows for doing so. These 14 LCPs have generated much discussion and debate among educators, and as such, have been very productive. Yet, at the same time, they seem far too broad and eclectic and are not focused upon significant issues of mind.

As with the learner-centred approach, constructivism has recently achieved some prominence as a theoretical foundation for teaching and leaning. We now turn to constructivist approaches to better understand collaborative tool learning.

CONSTRUCTIVISM

Constructivism is a recent perspective or philosophy on learning with ancient roots that has extensive implications for the use of collaborative learning tools. In employing constructivism, some teachers believe that better learning occurs when knowledge is the result of a situated construction of reality. Unfortunately, although constructivist revolutionaries have ventured onto the battlefield of epistemological change, most have not provided practicing educators with the wherewithal to reconstitute and embed constructivist ideas within their personal philosophies and teaching practices.

Teachers might, in fact, design useful constructivistic learning environments and strategies, but may not recognise that they operate from a constructivist paradigm. Even when constructivism is recognised as valuable, few guidelines exist for implementing and assessing it. So, when CSCL tools enter the instructional arsenal of public schools and higher education settings, constructivism may not be the theory of choice. And, undoubtedly, many scholars and researchers fuel this problem with intense debates that most practitioners simply lack the time and energy to deal with.

Further muddying the debate, there is no canonical form of constructivist theory. Two variations-cognitive constructivist and social constructivist-and there are undoubtedly more. Cognitive constructivists tend to draw insight from Piaget and focus on individual constructions of knowledge discovered in interaction with the environment. Here try to clarify some of the distinct differences in teaching practices between these two positions as well as some of the more subtle ones, which are really more a matter of emphasis than epistemological divergence.

It is worth pointing out that collaborative learning tools can be used from both a cognitive constructivist and social constructivist perspective. CSCL tools can place students in an authentic learning situation wherein an assortment of primary data and human resources are at their fingertips. A wealth of Internet and local area network tools, in fact, are now available in many public schools and universities to offer students significant opportunities to explore personal interests and expand on prior experiences.

Moreover, many technology tools enable teachers to structure learning activities that address student misconceptions, seek student elaboration of their answers, and pose questions. Perhaps, even more importantly, a few educators have come to recognise the importance of social constructivism for electronic learning because the potential for collaboration and negotiation embedded within it provides the learner with the opportunity to obtain alternative perspectives on issues and offer personal insights; in effect, to engage in meaning making and knowledge negotiation. When CSCL tools are developed and used from a social constructivist viewpoint, new communities of learning often emerge.

Whereas cognitive constructivists focus on making learning more relevant, building on student prior knowledge, posing contra-dictions, and addressing misconceptions, social constructivists emphasise human dialogue, interaction, negotiation, and collaboration. Across both viewpoints, constructivistic educational practices and orientations emphasise active, generative learning, with curricula wherein teachers continue to perform a critical learning function as learning consultants and guides.

Tools fostering social interaction and learner-centred instructional practices are transforming learning from silent, solitary acts to lively, meaning-making events rich in discussion and interchange. Sociocultural theory and social constructivist teaching practices provide the backbone for such leadership.

SOCIO-CULTURAL VIEWS

As worldwide learning forums or educational "networlds" arise, the resulting electronic interactions between humans should be investigated through suitable social and cultural lenses. A primary tenet of Vygotskian psychology is that individual mental functioning is inherently situated in social interactional, cultural, institutional, and historical contexts. Therefore, to understand human thinking and learning, one must examine the context and setting in which that thinking and learning occurs.

Mediation: The tools and signs one is exposed to, therefore, influence or mediate new patterns of thought and mental functioning. One repercussion is that intelligence is no longer viewed as static, but dynamic. Mediational tools and signs could be mathematical symbols, artwork, or diagrams as well as software visualisations, electronic messages, WWW course homepages and student conferences, and other electronically displayed information.

The critical point here is that as technology advances to alter cultural tools and institutional settings, the available mediational means that can impact cognitive functioning also change. Given the technological changes we have experienced in recent years, there are undoubtedly a myriad of untapped human-learning possibilities from a sociocultural point of view.

Zone of Proximal Development: According to socio-cultural theorists, an individual acquires new mental functions and patterns of thought from the mediational assistance of tools, signs, and human scaffolding when it is offered within his or her zone of proximal development. The ZPD as the distance between a child's independent problem-solving level and that obtained under adult guidance or in collaboration with more capable peers.

ZPDs, therefore, depend on the quality of the total interactive context as well as individual learner capabilities. A ZPD might be evident in online communities when students teach their peers about their particular region or locale as well as when the teaching comes directly from a computer tool in the form of thinking-related prompts and feedback mechanisms.

Such computer prompts embed strategies intended to be internalised by the learner. The resulting intellectual benefits from electronic collaboration with peers, teachers, and technology tools may rest, however, on the extent of student reflection and general "mindfulness" during these learning collaborations and collective knowledge-building experiences.

Internalisation: Central to the premise of ZPDs, and sociocultural theory itself, is Vygotsky's suggestion that higher mental functioning is dependent on the process of internalisation. From a Vygotskian perspective, electronic social interaction utilises, extends, and creates ZPDs to foster learner skills and capacities that originally were active only in collaborative or assisted learning situations, but gradually become internalised as independent self-regulatory processes.

In other words, internalisation has occurred when processes first performed with others on a social plane are successfully executed by a learner in an independent learning activity. And how do learners, or sets of learners, within this internalisation process, appropriate the new skills and information initially encountered on the social plane for their own unique needs.

Cognitive Apprenticeship: In asserting that learning is most effective when it approximates real-world situations or problem scenarios, sociocultural research on collaborative technology also draws on insights from cognitive apprenticeship theory.

As mentors negotiate and support novice learners through experiences suitable to their ZPDs, they, in turn, gradually cede control of the task to the student. When the learning participants gradually assume greater task responsibility, they begin to internalise standard cultural practices. Such apprenticing situations and activities do not always imply vertical "teacher-to-student" relationships, however. Teachers may, in fact, assume colearner or coparticipant role in some of these learning situations, whereas their role in others may center on performance feedback and review.

A rationale for at least six teaching methods of these cognitive apprenticeships:

— Modeling,

— Coaching,

— Scaffolding and fading,

— Articulation,

— Reflection, and

— Explorations, which are briefly defined next.

Assisted Learning. Not only is the environment transformed when adopting sociocultural practices, but so, too, is the pedagogical role of the teacher. Clearly, the focus here is on assisting learning, not directing it. According to Tharp, adept sociocultural teaching is responsive in nature; instead of assigning tasks, relying on text readings, and fostering standard practices, sociocultural teachers value assisting or supporting the performance of their students.

Tharp further argued that there are seven basic ways for teachers to "assist" in the learning process:

a) Modeling,

b) Feedback,

c) Contingency management,

d) Instructing,

e) Cognitive structuring,

f) Questioning, and

g) Task structuring.

Merging these seven forms of learning assistance with six cognitive apprenticeship techniques, mentioned above, renders the following socio-culturally based teaching techniques:

a) Modeling to illustrate performance standards and verbalise invisible processes,

b) Coaching to observe and supervise students, thereby guiding them toward expert performance,

c) Scaffolding and fading to support what learners cannot yet do and gradually removing that support as competence is displayed,

d) Questioning to request a verbal response from learners while supporting them with mental functions they cannot produce alone,

e) Encouraging student articulation of their reasoning and problem-solving processes,

f) Pushing student exploration and application of their problem-solving skills,

g) Fostering student reflection and self-awareness (e.g., through performance replays),

h) Providing cognitive task structuring by explaining and organising the task within students' ZPDs,

i) Managing instruction with performance feedback and positive reinforcement, and

j) Using direct instruction to provide clarity, needed content, or missing information.

When these means of assistance are woven together, the teaching-learning situation evolves into a rich "instructional conversation". By using this instructional framework to imagine rich, interactive conversations among students and teachers and beyond, we are optimistic that CSCL technologies can provide effective learning assistance within learner ZPDs.

Tele-apprenticeship: In merging the aforementioned strategies with global networking technologies for "tele-apprenticeship", many universities and public schools are exploring CSCL tool features that provide unprecedented student-student social interaction opportunities and momentous cross-cultural activities and events.

Now, online apprenticeships can involve experts and peers demonstrating ideas, posing questions, offering insights, and providing relevant information when needed. Recent breakthroughs in videoconferencing tools showcase such authentic avenues for student and instructor social interaction and dialogue.

A series of CSCL breakthroughs, in fact, have resulted in fully accredited online PhD programmes, which feature electronic file exchange, e-mail office hours, electronic libraries, virtual cafes, whiteboards, debates and opinion polls, role-taking activities, and student dialogue transcripts. Such tools and strategies collectively function to electronically apprentice and assist in student learning.

Another celebrated example of a cognitive apprenticeship is to involve students in genuine scientific data collection and reporting about the weather. Along these same lines, the Internet to build communities of physics teachers who then apprenticed less skilled learners through a mix of microcomputer laboratory activities and electronic sharing of results with students and teachers at other locales.

Scaffolded Instruction: Such cognitive apprenticeships are, of course, inherently reliant on a mentor or guide who effectively uses "scaffolded instruction." In selecting scaffolded instruction, a mentor or guide provides the learner with the support or assistance necessary to complete a task that would not have been completed without the help. Examples of this support might include prompts, hints, comments, explanations, questions, counter examples, and suggestions.

A learning scaffold may be embedded in an explicit request to include additional information or a more general question or comment intended to spur new idea linkages or course connections. Of course, these learning aids are faded and removed as the learner assumes control over the activity. Through such assistance, the learner (or a team of learners) solves a problem, generates solutions, and gains insights that would ordinarily rest beyond his or her independent abilities.

In terms of such scaffolded learning activities, collaborative technologies can offer opportunities for both peer and mentor electronic guidance and feedback that stimulate student discussion and internal reflection. Experts might also provide electronic demonstrations and task assistance. Such electronic tool support and scaffolded assistance is especially important for young children because the support structure aiding the acquisition of oral communication, which has developed over many thousands of years, is not available for young readers and writers.

Until recently, reading and writing were strangely removed forms of communication not necessarily driven by human interaction; they simply involved a mark-making process that required explicit awareness of metalinguistic aspects of language. Unfortunately, reading and writing literacies do not develop spontaneously from spoken language; they are inaccessible to consciousness without the aid of a literate partner or guide.

For young children, this means that, unlike their speech system, when reading or writing, there are no outside others to support and provide feedback on their communicative ability. Therefore, that electronic tools not only might enhance literacy guidance possibilities, but extensive research in this area might inform socio-cultural theorists of the types and conditions of effective teacher and mentor guidance and scaffolding.

Inter-subjectivity: According to the socio-cultural perspective, scaffolded instruction is bound to be more effective when the players of the learning situation experience inter-subjectivity. As learners find common ground or shared thoughts, they can more easily exchange their ideas, build new knowledge, and negotiate meanings. Not surprisingly, the country to find and document collaborative communication tools, he discovered that the most promising ones were those that created a mental "shared space". These communication tools promote new forms of social interaction and productivity.

In addition to the many apprenticeship possibilities, therefore, electronic conferencing tools open up new avenues for students to take the perspective of peers and better understand their expectations and potential reactions. In moving beyond local area networks, global networks and associated curricula bring new audiences to young learners. There are a wealth of instructional design possibilities and pedagogical strategies for fostering electronic perspective taking.

Computer conferencing and collaboration technologies, for instance, might encourage learners to consider alternative perspectives and viewpoints by providing expert feedback windows, interactive debate forums, juxtapositions of opinions, scrollable dialogue-tracking devices, private reflection notes, peer commenting windows, public text-pointing devices, and interactive prompts available on demand.

These are the types of tools that need to be developed and tested to help egocentric or culturally unaware students decenter from their own narrow points of view and engage in extensive dialogue with their peers. Such tools not only bring unique opportunities for enhancing perspective taking and inter-subjectivity, but, in fact, provide a glimpse into the entire "activity" of electronic collaboration.

Activity Setting as Unit of Analysis: From a socio-cultural perspective, the lifeblood of new intellectual functioning is, in fact, the activity setting. It is from activity settings that one can simultaneously begin to understand groups or individuals, products or processes, and cognitions or cultures. Similarly, using human action as the primary unit of analysis because it helps one understand the socio-cultural context as well as the mental functioning of individuals operating within it.

Ideas about activity settings have penetrated psychological research in a variety of domains, including early literacy in the home, classroom learning, after-school computer play environments, and even workplace settings such as navy vessels and medical practices.

The mind rarely works alone and the mind "can be said to extend beyond the skin", indicate that thinking in such settings is distributed. Accordingly, by attempting to understand activity settings, the focus of evaluation has shifted from individual mental functioning to groups of minds in interaction.

Distributed Intelligence in a Learning Community: Whereas an activity system includes subjects, rules, communities, objects, and divisions of labor, it is the tools that mediate the activity and connect humans to objects and other people. There are a myriad of CSCL tools to create new forms of activity settings for both human-human and human-computer interaction and collaboration. The current generation of collaborative educational learning tools present unique opportunities for supporting and organising human conversations and creating new communities of learning.

Because human mental functioning is rooted in social relations and intellectual performance is distributed among members of a learning community, it is critical to begin to understand how electronic tools might enhance the collective intelligence of such a community. When socio-cultural theory is finally merged with electronic tool development and use, the answers to these questions may arise in rich, instructional conversations among learning participants wherein new meanings and insights are coconstructed and debated. Certainly that should be the benchmark for this field.

Collaborative technologies is in a prime position to test and extend sociocultural theory, many questions and issues remain. For instance, if the mind is distributed in society, then the tools for collaboration should offer a unique way to illustrate this in action. Second, if cultural artifacts and institutions underpin human development, then we need to grasp unique opportunities for human development as new collaborative educational learning tools spring forth and intersect. Instead of simply purchasing the latest CSCL tools and systems, therefore, one must first grasp their utility as scaffolded learning devices.

Even the social context of extremely popular instructional techniques, such as using a word processor for collaborative writing, for instance, are only beginning to be documented and better understood. In terms of activity settings, collaborative tools should also offer interesting windows on the negotiation of meaning and learner interaction. If the interaction with experts and more capable peers on a social plane leads to student intellectual growth and new competencies, then we need to create and test electronic situations wherein students represent and share knowledge.

In order to test whether development moves from the external to the internal plane, the activities appearing within collaboration tools must be later seen in students' independent problem-solving acts. And, if speech is a bridge for movement from the external plane to new strategic behaviours, then the dialogue patterns of electronic social interaction as well as any ensuing journal writings and private reflections must be captured and inspected.

Still other sociocultural questions face collaborative learning tool advocates. For instance, if scaffolded instruction is important in moving students from novice to more expert like behaviour, then we need to create situations wherein the cognitive apprenticeship and dialogue possibilities of collaborative tools can be fostered and examined. Pedagogically intriguing electronic apprenticeship tools should allow for various types of learning assistance and social interaction. For instance, explicit displays of shared knowledge should foster greater participant inter-subjectivity and perspective taking.

In addition, then effective forms of electronic learning assistance and scaffolding need to be better understood. Finally, this field is in dire need of learning benchmarks, signposts, and standards. Certainly, new collaborative problem-solving or problem-finding assessments need to be developed and tested.

The appearance on a nearly daily basis of new interactive technologies has sorely taxed the ability of educators to conceptualise and capitalise upon the processes of learning and teaching in this brave new world. Familiar definitions of school, teacher, subject matter content, and so forth seem increasingly irrelevant in a world where access to information is expanding at explosive rates and where the ability to communicate on a global basis is as simple as pointing and clicking a screen icon. In response, learner-centred, constructivist, and socio-cultural models have arisen to place emphasis on guiding and supporting students as they construct their understanding of the cultures and communities of which they are a part.

In the process of shifting our attention to the knowledge-building and social negotiation activities of a learner in meaningful environments, we recognise the need to anchor learning in real-world or authentic contexts that give it meaning and purpose. Perhaps, even more important, we have come to recognise the significance of collaboration in learning when it provides opportunities to receive a myriad of alternative perspectives, test contrary ideas, and collect new data and insights.

This search for learner-centred, constructivist, and socio-cultural components of collaborative educational learning tools was in response to the dearth of theoretical grounding related to CSCL tools. Although our theoretical search indicates that useful components and connections are being made, more knowledge is desperately needed about the relevance, prevalence, and consequence of these innovative learning tools. For pedagogical progress to be made in electronic learning environments, educators must begin to realise that the lockstep factory model of education is out of sync with prevailing views of learning.

Today, with the complementary nature of socio-cultural theory and collaborative learning tools, learning is viewed as fundamentally social and derived from authentic engagement with others in a community of practice. Just where we are headed is uncertain given the tremors of change and parallel tension in the nature of learning and schooling in the 1990s. However, this uncertainty has been fostered, at least in part, by the emergence of CSCL tools and their associated learning activities.

What is clear is that recent advancements in collaborative tools parallel new developments in psychological theory on human teaching and learning. What is also apparent is that further inroads into the use of collaborative educational learning tools will help educational researchers design more powerful learning environments during the early stages of the next millennium.

The theoretical frameworks presented here—learner centred, constructivist, and socio-cultural—do overlap, we find most hope for CSCL developments within the latter. And while some perspectives emphasise such critical issues as meaningful learning, developing higher order thinking strategies, and encouraging learners to link new information to old, the social context of learning too often does not play a central enough role in these approaches.

In contrast, a sociocultural view on collaborative tools explicitly points to the social origin of higher mental functions, the distributed nature of learning and problem solving, and the importance of technology tools in mediating individual and cultural development.

8

STUDENT MOTIVATION

Student motivation refers to a student's willingness, need, desire and compulsion to participate in, and be successful in, the learning process. Students who are motivated to engage in school select tasks at the border of their competencies, initiate action when given the opportunity, and exert intense effort and concentration in the implementation of learning tasks; they show generally positive emotions during ongoing action, including enthusiasm, optimism, curiosity, and interest. Less motivated or disengaged students, on the other hand, are passive, do not try hard, and give up easily in the face of challenges.

Types of Motivation

Student motivation is often divided into two categories, Extrinsic motivation and Intrinsic motivation.

Extrinsic motivation: A student can be described as extrinsically motivated when he or she engages in learning "purely for the sake of attaining a reward or for avoiding some punishment". School practices that seek to motivate students extrinsically include publicly recognising students for academic achievements; giving out stickers, candy, and other rewards; and taking away privileges, such as recess, on the basis of students' academic performance.

Intrinsic motivation: A student can be described as intrinsically motivated when he or she is motivated from within: Intrinsically motivated students actively engage themselves in learning out of curiosity, interest, or enjoyment, or in order to achieve their own intellectual and personal goals. "A student who is intrinsically motivated... will not need any type of reward or incentive to initiate or complete a task. This type of student is more likely to complete the chosen task and be excited by the challenging nature of an activity".

While any kind of motivation seems preferable to none, there is compelling evidence that students who are more intrinsically than extrinsically motivated fare better. In fact, some research demonstrates that using extrinsic motivators to engage students in learning can both lower achievement and negatively affect student motivation. Students who are motivated to complete a task only to avoid consequences or to earn a certain grade rarely exert more than the minimum effort necessary to meet their goal. And, when students are focused on comparing themselves with their classmates, rather than on mastering skills at their own rate, they are more easily discouraged and their intrinsic motivation to learn may actually decrease. While external rewards sustain productivity, they "decrease interest in the task, thereby diminishing the likelihood that the task will be continued in the future".

Students who are intrinsically motivated, on the other hand, come out ahead in a number of areas. Intrinsically motivated students:

— Earn higher grades and achievement test scores, on average, than extrinsically-motivated students,

— Are better personally adjusted to school,

— Employ "strategies that demand more effort and that enable them to process information more deeply",

— Are more likely to feel confident about their ability to learn new material,

— Use "more logical information-gathering and decision-making strategies" than do extrinsically-motivated students,

— Are more likely to engage in "tasks that are moderately challenging, whereas extrinsically oriented students gravitate toward tasks that are low in degree of difficulty",

— Are more likely to persist with and complete assigned tasks,

— Retain information and concepts longer, and are less likely to need remedial courses and review,

— Are more likely to be lifelong learners, continuing to educate themselves outside the formal school setting long after external motivators such as grades and diplomas are removed.

It should be noted here that some researchers object to describing student motivation as either intrinsic or extrinsic. This division is too simple to reflect the many complex and interrelated factors that influence students' motivation to succeed in school. Most successful people are motivated by both internal and external factors, and suggest that educators build on both types when working to engage students more fully in school.

Most educators believe motivation is necessary for effective learning. Most know there are many sources of student motivation, and just about everyone wants students to be more motivated and engaged. One common perspective in research on student motivation is to identify student qualities that are conducive to engagement with learning. Investigations focus on what students bring to their learning by way of goals, values or purposes. Sometimes these variables are viewed as trait-like dispositions that apply across situations. Sometimes they are treated as variables that are context specific.

A second general approach starts with the proposition that learning conditions are critical. Certain types of schooling experiences promote motivation and engagement. From this perspective what is needed is more careful attention to designing and implementing conditions that maximise the opportunity for lively, challenging learning experiences. However, at the same time there are features of classrooms, peer groups, the tasks, and teachers that are known to trigger negative moods and anxiety, or values incompatible with learning. The result is boredom, disengagement, disruptive tactics and dropping out.

Motivation and engagement are essential for effective learning. Everyone knows it but it has not always been easy to demonstrate how they influence learning and achievement. One way of distinguishing these two concepts is to suggest that: "Motivation is about energy and direction, the reasons for behaviour, why we do what we do. Engagement describes energy in action; the connection between person and activity".

Current knowledge concerning students' motivation and engagement will be reviewed as it relates to two research perspectives: the person and the situation. From the person perspective, the issues concern variables that define a characteristic or set of characteristics identifying individual differences in reactivity, sometimes as broad dispositions, predispositions or orientations, sometimes as transient states. From the situational perspective the issues concern identification of specific contextual variables that trigger, support or increase student motivation and engagement. This perspective embraces research that is looking at broad, global variables such as school systems, whole-school environments, and classrooms as well as research that examines the effects of contextual variables represented by what happens in a single learning episode.

Research on motivation and engagement is also about the unmotivated and the disengaged. Over the last decade a number of reviews have drawn attention to the fact that young adolescents are often distinguished by their lack of connection with schooling. They are described as bored, disengaged, or, unmotivated.

MAJOR INTERNATIONAL PERSPECTIVES

Probably the most comprehensive international perspective on student motivation can be found in recent publications from the Programme for International Student Assessment (PISA) and the findings relate to the contribution of both individual (personal) and contextual (situational) factors. Studies sponsored by the OECD, have used a number of different indicators of student motivation ranging from measures of students' participation and sense of belonging at school, to self-report indicators of interest and attitudes within specific learning domains.

Reports from the PISA 2000 wave of data collection, refer to student engagement defining it in terms of 'belonging'; a "disposition towards learning, working with others and functioning in a social institution ... expressed in students' feelings that they belong at school and in their participation in school activities". Engaged students are those who value their relationships with peers and with teachers, and who see school as an important part of their life. On the other hand disengaged or disaffected students report feeling they do not belong and tend to dismiss schooling. One index of engagement used in PISA, participation, was measured using attendance records, and approximately 20% of students were classified as disengaged.

A second index defined as sense of belonging, was measured by self-report ratings, and approximately 25% of students were classified as disaffected. Similar prevalence estimates were found across most participating OECD countries. Participation, as used in this large-scale survey is a behavioural measure of engagement that focuses on the individual and along with the sense of belonging, represents individual differences in connection with schooling. The other side of these analyses was the identification of contextual factors that showed consistent associations with engagement. Consistently across the countries where data were collected, school climate was shown to be an important factor in students' engagement with schooling. The same PISA report indicated substantial within school variation in proportion of disaffected students. Students were "more likely to be engaged if they attend schools with high average socio-economic status, strong disciplinary climate, good student-teacher relations and high expectations for student success".

However, when issues of motivation and engagement are raised, often the concern is to identify the predictive effects for students' achievement. Again, looking to the international surveys of education, there has been wide dissemination of results concerning the relationship between engagement and reading literacy. Quoting again from PISA, engagement in reading activities is an important predictor of literacy achievement. In this case, engagement behaviour was measured by specific reading practices such as time spent on reading, and the diversity and content of reading.

Reading attitudes were also measured through self-report ratings on dimensions of interest in, and the value of reading. When engagement in reading was considered the outcome, home environment factors such as availability of books and cultural communication were important. School factors such as relationship with teacher and classroom climate also contributed. When students' engagement in reading was entered as a predictor of literacy achievement it was a stronger predictor than gender. Socio-economic status was a significant factor in literacy achievement but of particular importance was the predictive power of reading engagement in relation to socio-economic status.

Students from the "lowest occupational status but highly engaged in reading obtain higher average reading scores than students whose parents have high or medium occupational status but who report to be poorly engaged in reading". Again, both students' orientation to reading (the individual differences perspective), and the environmental supports for reading activities are important for strong reading achievement. The large-scale surveys have concentrated on behavioural indicators of engagement supported by some self-report measures of interest and attitudes toward specific achievement domains.

However, a large body of smaller-scale, school-based research has investigated motivation and engagement by identifying specific motivational variables and then investigating how these relate to students' behaviour and achievement. Mastery goals, performance goals, intrinsic motivation, self-efficacy, agency, individual interest, situational interest, curiosity, work avoidance, extrinsic motivation, learned helplessness, perceived competence, self-competence. All of these have been used to describe motivational aspects of students' connection with learning and predominantly represent the individual perspective. Some denote positive connection, others dis-connection or alienation from learning.

In recent years there have been a number of major reviews of the motivational research literature and in spite of the wide range of specific concepts and the fact that these concepts are often " fuzzy with no clear boundary definitions" there appears to be some convergence in their framing summaries. Murphy and Alexander classified the terms used in empirical motivation research reported in major publications over five years. Four basic groupings emerged:

— Goal concepts.

— Intrinsic and extrinsic motivation.

— Interest: individual interest, situational interest.

— Self-schema: agency, attribution, self-competence, self-efficacy.

Pintrich reviewed the same broad field and suggested that five general concepts describe what motivates students in classrooms.

— Adaptive self-efficacy and competence beliefs.

— Adaptive attributions and control beliefs.

— Higher levels of interest and intrinsic motivation.

— Higher levels of value.

— Goals.

A consistent picture emerges despite some difference in the precise separation into groupings. Murphy and Alexander separate intrinsic and extrinsic motivation from various forms of interest while Pintrich has grouped them as one category. On the other hand Murphy and Alexander list as one group a number of self-schema concepts which Pintrich has separated into efficacy and competence beliefs, and, attribution and control beliefs. Pintrich has included value in a separate category while Murphy and Alexander defined this area as being outside their purpose arguing that expectancy-value constructs developed by Eccles and colleagues are overarching constructs linking more specific motivational concepts.

Considerable research endeavour has gone into investigations of student engagement. A significant number of these research reports have focused on identifying how achievement goals influence achievement.

The linking of motivational and emotional variables as they might influence learning has some theoretical support from theories of emotion such as emotions are key motivational variables. At the most basic level, the appraisal processes that underpin emotions involve approach or avoidance reactions that direct subsequent processing. In similar vein, Boekaerts argues that motivation involves habitual behaviour (e.g., goal setting, general traits and domain-specific beliefs) while emotion involves students' current concerns. Therefore, in any specific learning context appraisal processes draw on both motivation and emotion to direct behaviour. The inclusion of emotion in these models is part of a theoretical shift that goes beyond research into learning and achievement. As part of the positive psychology school of thought, Fredrickson proposed a broaden-andbuild model of positive emotion to understand a wide range of behaviours including both educational and health-related settings:

Positive emotions (e.g., joy, interest, and contentment) broaden an individual's momentary thought-action repertoire, which in turn can build that individual's enduring personal resources, resources that also served the ancestral function of promoting survival. Positive emotions expand experience whether this is through giving more attention to an activity that has triggered interest or re-engaging with an enjoyable activity. Fredricksen identified interest as one of the major positive emotions. It "not only broadens an individual's momentary thought-action repertoire as the individual is enticed to explore, but over time and as a product of sustained exploration, interest also builds the individual's store of knowledge and cognitive abilities."

Interest opens the individual to new experience and brings them in direct contact with knowledge and experience that goes beyond their current level of achievement. In achievement settings positive activating emotions serve the function of maintaining connection with learning activities. Feeling interested in an activity leads to decisions and actions that efficacy and self-competence beliefs. Nor can it be described adequately without referring to the developmental patterns concerning beliefs about the relationship between ability and effort in learning and achievement.

MOTIVATION IN ADULT EDUCATION

The rationale for research into adult motivation for education and training rests firstly on the phenomenon of ever-growing demand for competence development, faced with stagnating, sometimes dwindling public and private funding of training. Caught in this double bind, trainers, HRD specia lists, managers and workers themselves have to find new ways of developing corporate knowledge and skills without necessarily banking on formal, subs idised training programmes. Hence the success of such concepts as informal learning, learning organisations, self-directed learning, work-based learning, etc. Hence also the increase in pressure on people's involvement in work performance and, consequently, in to the self-management of their qualif ications. Social and economic pressure on organisations thus "naturally" bring about questions of individual motivation to work and to learn in a more acute manner.

Secondly, over the last 25 years, most of the new practical developments in adult education have taken for granted the fact that adults are necessarily "volunteers for learning". What might have been obvious in a different social and historical context appears today as somewhat less sure, to say the least. Moreover, as new approaches to learning develop, more and more commitment is expected from learners themselves if any result is to be hoped for. Thus, adults are more and more "mobilised" to engage in training, but not necessarily "motivated" to learn. A "new educational deal" is this taking shape right before our eyes, which engages both researchers, experts and practitioners to have a second look at the field of motivation and action within the realm of adult education and learning.

Theoretical Model Presentation

On the theoretical side, human motivation considered as a "hypothetical construct used to describe external and internal forces that explain the start, strength, direction and persistence of action". According to this view, human motivation assessment must be regarded as a "snapshot" of the relations that establish themselves, at a given context, at a given time, between a person and her/his environment, or a part thereof. This concept of motivation drives us away from other theories that stress, in human action, the role of unique processes, whether they be an located within the individual or within her/his environment.

For instance, conventional behavioural and sociological theories on the one hand, psychoanalytic and strictly cognitive theories on the other, draw a firm line between the effects of external or internal processes, to the point of understating the other side of the equation. The first phase of the research led us to examine research production around the themes of adult motivation to learn, participation in adult education, and adult learning. This led us to discard the longstanding paradigms of human motivation and action and to concentrate on socio-cognitive psychology as the one research paradigm in tune with our interactive view of the problem.

Educational psychology has taught for long that motivation is an indispensable ingredient of learning. But motivation theories, until fairly recently, were of little help to understand and facilitate adult learning especially in French research with few, albeit noticeable exceptions. Today, with the development of socio-cognitive theories of learning and motivation, mostly in Anglo-American-oriented literature, adult educators may draw upon a large, consistent, theoretically sound body of research. A new vision of adult motivation for education and its impact on learning is thus slowly emerging. With the theoretical backing mentioned above, a model of adult motivation to engage in training was developed around two main components: a renewed pattern of motives, and a threefold vision of motivational processes.

Adults motives for participating in adult education seem to follow four major orientations, derived from Houle's initial vision and organised on two axes.

a) Along a first axis, motives are orientated towards intrinsic versus extrinsic orientations.
b) On a second axis, motives are orientated towards learning versus participating (in the first case, a motive is geared towards the acquisition of knowledge or skill; in the second case, a motive is geared towards other objectives, such as having a good time, making money, or escaping some boring activity).

The combination of these orientations and axes, combined with empirical analysis of adult motives to engage in training, produces 10 specific motives which were labeled as follows. One is both intrinsic and learning-oriented ("epistemic"); two are both intrinsic and participation-oriented ("social-affective" and "hedonic"). Three are extrinsic and participation-oriented ("economic", "derivative," "prescribed"); two are extrinsic and learning-oriented ("personal-operational", "professional-operational"). Two are extrinsic and either participation or learning-oriented ("vocational", "identity-based").

It is worth underlining the fact that motives form temporary patterns of motivation that cannot be assimilated to either permanent dimensions of the self, or to lasting indexes of an individual's "rapport" to training, or even to a stable characteristic of the person's motivation for a given learning content. Motives have three major characteristics here: they are plural, changeable and contingent upon the individual's life context.

The second aspect of the theoretical model was directly drawn from our analysis of educational psychology productions and their applicability to both our field and paradigm of research. Three concepts have thus been identified to complete our model. The theoretical construct of adult motivation to engage in training was established upon the combination of motives and the three following intertwined processes :

— Perceived competence (or self-efficacy), based on Bandura's sociocognitive view of human action.

— Self-determination, based on Deci's conceptualisation of motivation.

— Project-formulation, as formalised in Nuttin's theory of human motivation, including perceived instrumentality of action.

In order to put this model to the test, to produce comparative results among a variety of adults about to engage in training, and to analyse the relations between motivation and performance in adult training, an empirical research was carried out in three phases:

— *Qualitative survey*: 61 adults who were about to start a training programme were interviewed about the nature of their engagement in the project. After a pre-test series of interviews, a panel was built, drawing on 7 different training situations. Content analysis was carried out using a "double-blind" approach. The initial model was slightly modified and validated.

— *Instrument design*: a 143-item, Lickert-type instrument was designed, field tested and completed by 400 adults in two different training contexts, leading to a significantly reduced second version (69 items) with satisfactory internal validity.

— *Quantitative survey*: the second version of the instrument was then proposed to 2,500 adults in 9 different contexts. Statistical analyses were carried out and results were obtained in the following areas:

  — Variations of various aspects of motivation according to socio-demographic variables (age, gender, SPC, activity status, etc.)

  — Correlational analyses among different motivational variables (motives, perception of competence, self-determination, project formation)

  — Relation of initial motivation and final performance in training.

STRATEGIES FOR INCREASING MOTIVATION

School practices can and do affect a student's level of

motivation. Skinner and Belmont caution, however, that this may not always be for the better:

If left to run their typical course, teachers tend to magnify children's initial levels of motivation. This is fine for students who enter the classroom motivationally "rich"; they will "get rich." However, for students whose motivation is low, their typical classroom experiences may result in its further deterioration. To be sure, efforts to promote student motivation need not be directed solely at students who have low levels of motivation. All students (and all schools, for that matter) would benefit from higher levels of engagement and motivation to succeed. Following are suggestions for both teachers and administrators seeking to increase students' motivation to learn:

At the classroom level:

— Use extrinsic rewards sparingly. If extrinsic motivators are to be used, they are most effective when rewards are closely related to the task accomplished. Also, rewards should only be given when they are clearly deserved. Giving a prize for minimally successful work sends the message that minimum effort is acceptable, and the reward then becomes meaningless.

— Ensure that classroom expectations for performance and behaviour are clear and consistent. Help students understand the criteria for individual assignments by giving them examples of high-, average-, and low-level work and then providing an opportunity to discuss how each piece was evaluated.

— Make students feel welcome and supported. Elementary school students in particular need to feel that teachers are involved in their lives. Take time to get to know students, talk to them individually, and "express enjoyment in [your] interactions".

— Respond positively to student questions, and praise students verbally for work well done.

— Work to build quality relationships with students, especially those considered to be at-risk and without other positive adult interaction; this is a critical factor of student engagement that allows children to foster a sense of connection with school.

— Break large tasks into a series of smaller goals. Doing so prevents students from becoming overwhelmed and discouraged by lengthy projects.

— Promote mastery learning. "When a student completes an assignment that does not meet the expected criteria, give her or him one or more opportunities to tackle the task again, with guidelines on how to achieve the desired result".

— Evaluate student work as soon as possible after project completion, and be sure that feedback is clear and constructive.

— Evaluate students based on the task, not in comparison to other students.

At the school and district levels:

— Make increasing student motivation a priority in school reform and restructuring efforts.

— Create a school culture that emphasises the importance of academic achievement. Design schoolwide symbols to show students that learning is valuable and that the entire staff is invested in students' success.

— Model and communicate the value of lifelong learning.

— Develop a school climate that recognises individual differences, encourages creativity, and gives both teachers and students a sense of autonomy. Particularly important is allowing students and teachers to have some degree of control over teaching and learning.

— Support teachers' efforts to increase student motivation, encouraging student-centered learning and outcomes-based instruction. Additionally, recognise teachers' individual learning needs and be supportive of their continuing education and involvement in research.

— Provide and participate in professional development activities that deal with motivation, effective use of homework, and student engagement.

— Finally, develop ways to involve parents. Discuss the issue of motivation with parents, involve them in the school's efforts to increase student engagement, and "give them guidance in fostering motivation in their children".

MOTIVATING STUDENTS TO ENGAGE IN CLASS ACTIVITIES

It only makes sense that the more interesting an assignment is, the more likely students are to immerse themselves in the task and stick with it through completion. Even highly motivated students need schoolwork that actively engages them by building on their interests and prior knowledge. In general, students need work that develops their sense of competency, allows them to develop connections with others, gives them some degree of autonomy, and provides opportunities for originality and self-expression. The challenge teachers face, then, is to create a learning environment that attends to all or most of these needs. Following is a list of suggestions for designing more engaging in-class activities and increasing the amount of time students spend on task.

Ensure course materials relate to students' lives and highlight ways learning can be applied in real-life situations. Schoolwork should be meaningful to students outside the school building, as well as within. Students are more engaged in activities when they can build on prior knowledge and draw clear connections between what they are learning and the world they live in. They also need to feel that "school work is significant, valuable, and worthy of their efforts".

Allow students to have some degree of control over learning. This can be done in any number of ways, from giving students choices between different assignments, to minimising adult supervision over group projects, to letting students monitor and evaluate their own progress. This doesn't mean teachers must relinquish control of the classroom: "Even small opportunities for choice, such as whether to work with a partner or independently" give students a greater sense of autonomy.

Assign challenging but achievable tasks for all students, including at-risk, remedial, and learning disabled students. Tasks that seem impossible easily discourage learners, as do those tasks that are rote and repetitive. Remedial programmes that limit students to repetitive basic skills activities actually "prompt students' lack of engagement in their schoolwork and frequently result in limited achievement". Students need to feel successful and that they've earned success.

Arouse students' curiosity about the topic being studied. Some of the researchers sugests using the "mystery" approach, in which students are presented with fragmentary or contradictory information about a subject and are then asked to examine available evidence to develop their own hypotheses. This kind of activity also builds on students' needs for competence and autonomy, giving students an opportunity to direct inquiry and "discover for themselves."

Design projects that allow students to share new knowledge with others. When students do assignments that only the teacher will read, they are entering into a nonreciprocal relationship. More often than not, the teacher already knows and has no real need for the information the student is providing him or her. Projects are more engaging when students share what they are learning in reciprocal relationships, as in collaborative projects where each student's knowledge is needed by others in the group to complete an assignment. It is also important to note that, in addition to instructional practice, certain elements of the classroom environment, such as seating arrangements and student behaviour, will influence how long students remain on task and engaged in their work.

Some of the researchers suggest teachers consider the goals of individual activities when determining how to arrange seats in the classroom. In their research into on-task behaviour in secondand third-grade classrooms, they found that students remained engaged in learning longer when desks were arranged appropriately for the task at hand: U-shaped arrangements for class discussions, rows for test taking, etc.

HOMEWORK POLICY

Much of what has been said about making in-class work more engaging can also be said of homework: out-of-class assignments should have a clear purpose, should be relevant to students' lives, and should be at the same time challenging and manageable. Homework carries with it some added complications, though. Not only does successfully engaging in homework depend a great deal on students' home environment, but homework experiences may also have a significant impact on students' long-term attitudes toward school.

In recent years there has been much debate about the value of homework. While some parents and educators firmly believe that assigning homework is an important part of school, others call the practice into question. Some critics of homework observe that not all students go home to a quiet and supportive study environment, and thus have little chance of being successful with out-of-school assignments. Still others point out that homework may contribute significantly to students' negative attitudes toward school, particularly if it is a source of conflict between students and parents, or is linked to punishment and other consequences at school. Proponents of homework, on the other hand, argue that homework serves a number of purposes and can benefit students when used appropriately. The main purposes generally associated with homework are as follows:

— To give students a chance to "review and practice what they have learned".

— To prepare students for the next day's lesson.

— To provide opportunities to identify and learn to use resources, such as the library, the Internet, reference books, and other community resources.

— To allow for more in-depth exploration of topics than is possible during class time.

— To help students develop time management, study, and organisational skills.

As might be expected, the effectiveness of different types of homework varies according to students' age and ability level. Some of the studis found that homework raises achievement "substantially" for high school students, but only about half that for students in the middle grades.

This is not to say that homework doesn't benefit younger students in different ways. Other studies have found that homework is most useful for elementary school students when it focuses on developing study habits and organisational skills. If your school does not already have a homework policy in place, you might discuss this with other teachers and administrators.

Homework policies, which function to define a standard set of expectations for and beliefs about homework, can be shared and reviewed with students, parents, and teachers at the beginning of each school year. At minimum, homework policies should define the role of homework in learning at each grade level, and the specific responsibilities of teachers, parents, and students.

While some educators caution that school and districtwide policies for homework can become restrictive, there are advantages to having a shared understanding of how homework is being used to support learning. Homework policies not only help define parents' role in homework, but also ensure that students and parents are informed about teachers' expectations. Another benefit of homework policies is that they allow teachers to develop a consistent, schoolwide set of expectations for students, which is particularly helpful for students who have several different teachers throughout the day. Developing a homework policy is also a good way for educators to get together, review the research, and explore how homework can best be used to promote achievement and engagement in school.

Role of Parents

Active parent involvement has been associated with numerous benefits for students, including increasing student motivation and engagement in school. When it comes to homework, though, parent involvement can take many different shapes, not all of which have a positive impact on learning. When working to increase student engagement and motivation, it is important to include parents and discuss ways they can support their children's learning both at school and at home.

First, it is important that parents understand what role teachers expect them to play, especially in terms of homework. What one parent views as helping out, a teacher might perceive as interference or cheating. And what a teacher might take for granted that parents can do-such as signing off on homework or checking spelling words-a parent may not have the skills or the time to follow through on. Clearly, it is important to communicate with parents about how to best help children learn. It is also necessary for educators to be sure their expectations are realistic, given parents' skills and schedules. It is equally important to be clear with parents about what kinds of involvement are actually beneficial to students. Studies have shown that parents who offer rewards for grades, or who punish students for poor performance, may actually decrease students' motivation to do well.

Fear of punishment, anxiety about meeting parents' expectations, and worrying about being compared to siblings not only cause stress for students, but can also detract from their intrinsic motivation and interest in learning. This is not to say that parents shouldn't be invested in how their children are doing in school. Rather, it suggests that there are more productive ways for them to be involved and show their interest in students' progress. To help children be successful with work at home and at school, parents can:

— Create a place at home that is conducive to studying. Good study environments are well-lit and quiet. Although every child's learning style is different, most educators agree that students do best when the television is off and the student is free from distractions.

— Set aside a specific time for homework each day. This might involve limiting television-watching or phone calls until homework is finished. Parents should be careful, though, not to pit homework against activities students enjoy, or to create situations in which students rush through their work in order to get back to other activities. Family routines-which include set homework times-have been linked to higher student achievement.

— Make sure students have all the supplies they need. Parents should check in with students ahead of time about the kinds of projects they will be doing: It might be tough to find a calculator or a report cover at 9:00 the night before an assignment is due.

— Be available if students have questions. Parents can support their children by looking over homework and giving suggestions, but should not do the homework for them.

— Make an effort to communicate regularly with teachers. If necessary, parents should ask teachers to clarify their expectations. It is also a good idea to find out ahead of time what kinds of resources-such as tutors or services for second language students-are available to students if they need help.

— Avoid linking rewards or punishment to school performance. While it is important for parents to recognise students' achievements, they should avoid external motivators for performance. Instead, parents should emphasise the value of learning and show they appreciate their child's hard work.

9

HUMAN-COMPUTER RELATIONSHIPS

Relationships are also fundamentally social and emotional; thus, detailed knowledge of human social psychology-with a particular emphasis on the role of affect-must be incorporated into these agents if they are to effectively leverage the mechanisms of human social cognition in order to build relationships in the most natural manner possible. The development of relational agents draws heavily from two existent threads of work in HCI (Human Computer Interaction): natural multi-modal interfaces (including embodied conversational agents and robots, and studies of computers as social actors.

People primarily build relationships in the context of face-to-face conversation thus, most of the relationship-building strategies discussed in the social sciences literature are most directly implementable as verbal or nonverbal conversational behaviours. This requires, at a minimum, some kind of natural conversational interface and, at a maximum, the use of embodied conversational agents, robots, or some other articulate physical form factor to enact both verbal and nonverbal communicative actions.

Social actors paradigm has demonstrated that people respond in social ways to computers (and other media) when provided with the appropriate social cues, even though they are typically unconscious of this behaviour. To date, most of the agents that have been developed to have relational behaviours, are systems built to support such short-term studies, and have been (intentionally) very simple implementations from a technical standpoint. Examples of some of the relational effects found by these studies are that people tend to like computers more when the computers flatter them, match their personality, or use humor.

However, nobody has investigated any long-term effects of such techniques, especially whether the benefits can be sustained over multiple interactions. The long-term concern is of special significance because of many users' experience with the well-known Microsoft Office Assistant. Clearly, the assistant did well in short-term evaluations or it wouldn't have been brought to market. Yet it is no secret that many users feel outrage toward this character upon repeated interaction. One way to get insight into the problem is to consider an "equivalent" human-human interaction.

Imagine an individual that shows up in your office uninvited, with no introduction, barging in when you are busy. He offers useless advice while projecting the image of being helpful, and then proceeds to ignore your initially polite expressions of annoyance. This character persists in trying to help despite that you increase the clarity of your emotional expression. Finally you have to tell the character explicitly to leave, which he eventually does, but first he gives you a wink and a little dance.If this behaviour were that of a human office assistant, then he would eventually be fired, or at least severely marginalised.

A range of applications for relational agents can begin to be delimited by investigating the range of things that human relationships are good for. Provision models of relationships in social psychology give an idea of the possibilities. Some of the types of support that relationships have been found to provide are: emotional support (e.g., esteem, reassurance of worth, affection, attachment, intimacy), appraisal support (e.g., advice and guidance, information, feedback), instrumental support (e.g., material assistance), group belonging, opportunities to nurture, autonomy support, and social network support (e.g., providing introductions to other people).

A large amount of empirical work has been done in social psychology and other fields that demonstrate a significant association between social support and health and survival. In addition to general health and well-being, social support has also been shown to play a significant role in adjustment to specific illnesses, such as cancer and cardiovascular disease. Some of the features of relationships that have been hypothesised to lead to health benefits include: provision of physical and emotional security, establishment of a frame of reference for social reality, normative and informational social influence, and cooperative goal-directed activity.

Health and well-being may also be augmented simply because relationships are emotionally gratifying. Relational agents could play a significant role in helping individuals- especially those in acute need (e.g., suffering from an illness and not having any human support network)--cope with their illnesses, and maintain high levels of well-being.

For better or for worse, relationships can also play a role in persuasion. Trustworthiness and likableness of a source of potentially persuasive information play a significant role in the Elaboration Likelihood Model of persuasion. In this theory, if a decision is of low personal importance then source characteristics-such as trustworthiness and likableness of the source of information- have a significant influence on the decision. However, if the outcome of the decision is of high personal importance then these factors have little or no influence on the outcome.

Thus, relational agents could be used, for example, as salespeople, which attempt to build relationships with their clients just as good human salespeople do. Some researchers of personal relationships have also defined interpersonal "closeness" as the degree to which relational partners influence each others' behaviour.

Within elementary school education, students' feelings of relatedness to their teacher and classmates have been found to be strong predictors of their cognitive, behavioural, and emotional engagement in classroom activities. In addition, there is evidence that relationships between students are important in peer learning situations, including peer tutoring and peer collaborative learning methodologies. Collaboration between friends involved in these exercises has been shown to provide a more effective learning experience than collaboration between acquaintances.

Friends have been shown to engage in more extensive discourse with one another during problem solving, offer suggestions more readily, and are more supportive and more critical than non-friends. In at least one experiment, friends worked longer on the task and remembered more about it afterwards than non-friends.

Even in areas in which the more personal, non-task-oriented, aspects of relationships are downplayed, there is evidence that relationships play an important role in task outcomes. One example of such an area is the world of corporate bureaucracy. Even here, the development of a network of interpersonal relationships has been found to be critical to a general manager's ability to implement his or her agenda, and the quality of these relationships has been found to be a key determinant of managerial effectiveness.

Subordinates reporting good relationships with superiors have been found to be better performers, assume more responsibility and contribute more to their units than those reporting poor relationships. The results also indicate that a service relationship with a particular human service provider is significantly more effective at engendering trust, commitment and referrals than attempts to establish brand or firm loyalty.

Finally, although some level of trust is important in all human-computer and human-human interactions, trust and engagement are especially crucial in applications in which a change in the user is desired and which require significant cognitive, emotional or motivational effort on the part of the user. In the helping professions-including clinical psychology, counseling, and coaching-there is a well-documented association between the quality of professional-client relationship and outcomes.

The positive effect of a good therapist-patient relationship on psychotherapeutic outcomes has been demonstrated in several studies, and has even been hypothesised to be the common factor underlying the many diverse approaches to psychotherapy that seem to provide approximately equal results. Thus, computer agents that function in helping roles, especially in applications in which the user is attempting to undergo a change in behaviour or cognitive or emotional state, could be much more effective if they first attempted to build trusting, empathetic relationships with their users.

A number of instruments have been developed for use in clinical psychotherapy to measure the quality of the client-therapist relationship. One of the most common measures in the literature is the Working Alliance Inventory, which measures the trust and belief that the therapist and patient have in each other as team-members in achieving a desired outcome. This inventory (and similar measures) has been used in therapy to assess the impact of the alliance on problems as wide-ranging as alcoholism, depression, drug use, and personality disorders, and has been demonstrated to have a significant correlation with outcome measures ranging from percentage of days abstinent, drinks per drinking day, and treatment participation for alcoholism, to employment and compliance with medication, to more general measures such as premature termination, Global Assessment Scale, MMPI, and many, many others.

SOCIAL PSYCHOLOGY OF PERSONAL RELATIONSHIPS

Dyadic Models

Most recent work in the social psychology of personal relationships takes a fundamentally dyadic approach to the concept of "relationship". This concept as referring to two people whose behaviour is interdependent, in that a change in the state of one will produce a change in the state of the other. Thus, a relationship does not reside in either partner alone, but in their interaction with each other. Further, a relationship is not defined exclusively by generic patterns of interaction, but by the unique patterns of interaction for a particular dyad.

This objective view of relationship as a pattern of interaction is also echoed in a recent study of peoples' relationships with the man-made objects in their environment. According to this study, much of the past work in psychology on the nature of people's interactions with objects has mostly been concerned with objects as symbolic representations for the self, for others, or for relationships e.g., Freud, Jung, and even Winnicott's treatment of "transitional objects", but are not at all concerned with the actual experience that people have with concrete objects in the world or their sense of connection to them.

Provision Models

The objective view of relationship in social psychology to characterise relationships in terms of what the people in them provide for one another.

- — Belonging and a sense of "reliable alliance". The existence of a bond that can be trusted to be there for a partner when they need it.
- — Emotional integration and stability. Friendships provide necessary anchor points for opinions, beliefs and emotional responses.
- — Opportunities for each partner to talk about themselves. Friendships help fulfill the need for self-expression and self-disclosure.

Provision of physical, psychological and emotional support. Physical support involves doing favors, such as giving someone a ride or washing the dishes. Psychological support involves showing appreciation for the other and letting them know their opinions are valued. Emotional support includes affection, attachment and intimacy.

Re-assurance of worth and value, and an opportunity to help others. We value friends because of their contribution to our self-evaluation and self-esteem, directly via compliments and indirectly by telling us of the good opinions of others. Also, friends increase our self-esteem by simply attending to us, by listening, asking our advice and valuing our opinions.

Economic Models

Incorporating the notion of relational provisions, economic models of relationship, such as social exchange theory, model relationships in terms of costs and benefits. These models are not strictly objective in that rather than being based on actual provisions, they are based on perceived benefits, costs, investments in and alternatives to a relationship, by the individuals in the relationship, and relate these factors to desire to stay in the relationship. Social exchange models have received more empirical validation than any other theoretical framework in the social psychology of personal relationships.

Dimensional Models

Perhaps the most common way of representing a relationship in the social sciences is with the use of dimensional models, which attempt to abstract the characteristics of a given relationship to a point in a small-dimensional Euclidean space. The most commonly used dimensions are power and social distance. Power refers to the ability of one individual to control the resources of another. Social distance refers to the dimension that differentiates between strangers and intimates at its extremes, and has been further decomposed into as many as 14 sub-dimensions. Other dimensions used to characterise relationships include equal and unequal, hostile and friendly, superficial and intense, and informal and formal.

While abstracting away from specific patterns of behaviour, these models often attempt to characterise the notion of 'connectedness' present in relationships through dimensions such as solidarity and affect. The literature on trust spans the disciplines of sociology, social psychology, and philosophy. Social psychologists have defined trust as "people's abstract positive expectations that they can count on partners to care for them and be responsive to their needs, now and in the future," and one model of the development of trust describes it as "a process of uncertainty reduction, the ultimate goal of which is to reinforce assumptions about a partner's dependability with actual evidence from the partner's behaviour".

Stage Models

In addition to models that capture a steady-state snapshot of a relationship, some researchers have attempted to develop "stage models", which assume there are a fixed set of stages that different types of relationships go through. For example, one model hypothesises that all relationships go through four stages: initial rapport; mutual self-revelation; mutual dependency; and personal need fulfillment. Stage models are now generally considered to provide very weak predictive power given their assumption of a fixed sequence of stages, since actual relationships often jump around among various stages in a non-linear manner.

People use myriad behaviours to establish and maintain relationships with each other, most of which could be used by computer agents to manage their relationships with their users. One distinction that can be made in delineating these behaviours is between those used to establish or change a relationship (such as small talk or getting acquainted talk and those used to maintain an on-going relationship (e.g., continuity behaviours, such as partners talking about what they did during times apart.)

Another distinction made by many researchers is between routine and strategic relational behaviours, with strategic behaviours being those intentionally used to manage a relationship (e.g., talking about the relationship) while routine behaviours are those people engage in for other reasons but which serve to maintain a relationship as a side effect (e.g., simply engaging in everyday tasks together on an on-going basis). Routine interactions with a computer thus can be seen as contributing to a relationship, even when no relational skills have been explicitly designed into the machine.

Relational Communication

Most human relationships are constructed in the context of faceto-face conversation. All language can be seen as carrying (at least) two kinds of meaning: propositional information of the sort studied in classical semantics, and relational information commenting on the nature of the relationship between the speaker and hearer and the attitude of the former towards the latter.

Thus, all forms of talk can be seen as instrumental in negotiating the relationship between interlocutors, and talk that is particularly lacking in task-oriented propositional content is often referred to as 'social dialogue' (also known as 'small talk' or 'phatic communion'). For example, the social greeting of "good morning" has lost much of its semantic meaning, but whether or not you choose to say it, as well as how you say it, can influence the development of a relationship. Social dialogue can be used to maintain a relational dial-tone even when no explicit task is being performed (the "phatic" function of utterances.

Of course, merely conducting social dialogue tends to establish rapport between interlocutors by increasing familiarity and establishing common ground between them (Malinowski 1923). Thus, for many computer applications, simply engaging a user and keeping them engaged-even when not performing a task-will help to establish a bond with the system.

The encoding of relational status in language is a phenomenon known as 'social deixis' and has been extensively studied in pragmatics and socio-linguistics. A familiar example in English is the form of address and greeting and parting routines that are used between people having different relationships, with titles ranging from professional forms to first names and greetings ranging from a simple "Hello" to the more formal "Good Morning", etc. Another example is politeness theory, which prescribes different forms of indirectness for a request given how burdensome the request is and the nature of the relationship between the requestor and requestee.

There are many other types of social deixis, especially in other languages that encode many different relational features including power, social distance, kinship relations, clan membership, and others. Thus, the appropriate use of social deixis can serve to ratify and maintain the status of an existing relationship, while using language features indicative of a different form of relationship can signal a desire to make a change in relational status. Thus, the forms of language used in a computer application, even it is only in menus or text messages, signals a certain set of relational expectations on the part of the user.

Relational Dynamics

Given the definition of relationship as patterns of interaction, one way people can change their relationship is by simply performing new activities together. However, this must be achieved through a negotiation in which both parties agree to the new activity. Since rejections are normally a threat to both party's self-esteem, people engage in elaborate routines to negotiate new activities so that they can ask without appearing to ask.

Another strategy for maintaining a relationship that is particularly relevant for HCI is meta-relational communication. This "talk about the relationship" is particularly important in the early stages of a relationship to clearly establish expectations when things are in transition, but is also important to periodically ensure that everything is going all right. Just imagine if computer systems could periodically check in with their users to ask how everything is going and offer to make changes every few weeks; the mere act of asking would demonstrate concern and caring for the user.

Empathy-the process of attending to, understanding, and responding to another person's expressions of emotion-is one of the core processes in building and maintaining relationships. This isn't true just for intimate relationships; it is cited as one of the most important factors in building good working alliances between helpers and their clients, and in physician-patient interactions it has also been shown to play a significant role in effecting prescription compliance and reducing patient complaints. Empathy is a prerequisite for providing emotional support which, in turn, provides "the foundation for relationship-enhancing behaviours, including accommodation, social support, intimacy, and effective communication and problem solving".

Even though computers can't demonstrate true empathy since they don't yet have the capacity for real feelings, As long as a computer appears to be empathetic and is accurate in its feedback, that it can achieve significant behavioural effects on a user, similar to what would be expected from genuine human empathy. There are many other strategies described in the literature for decreasing social distance along various dimensions:

— Reciprocal deepening self-disclosure increases trust, closeness and liking, and has been demonstrated to be effective in text-based human-computer interactions.

— Use of humor is cited as an important relationship maintenance strategy and has been demonstrated to increase liking in human-computer interaction.

— Talking about the past and future together and reference to mutual knowledge are cited as the most reliable cues people use to differentiate talk between strangers and acquaintances.

— Continuity behaviours to bridge the time people are apart (appropriate greetings and farewells and talk about the time spent apart) are important to maintain a sense of persistence in a relationship.

— Emphasising commonalities and de-emphasising differences is associated with increased solidarity and rapport. This can also be achieved indirectly through the process of mirroring in which one person adopts some aspects of the other's behaviour. "Lexical entrainment"- using a partner's words to refer to something-is a technique used by helpers to build rapport with clients.

Nonverbal behaviour in face-to-face conversation can also play a significant role in relationship management. One of the most consistent findings on the nonverbal display of interpersonal attitudes is that the use of "immediacy" behaviours-including close conversational distance, direct body and facial orientation, forward lean, increased and direct gaze, smiling, pleasant facial expressions and facial animation in general, nodding, frequent gesturing and postural openness-projects liking for the other and engagement in the interaction, and is correlated with increased solidarity.

There is empirical evidence that while such non-verbal behaviour may not be very important in task-oriented interactions, it is much more important in interactions that are more social in nature. In a review of studies comparing video and audio-mediated communication, Whittaker and O'Conaill concluded that video was superior to audio only for social tasks while there was little difference in subjective ratings or task outcomes in tasks in which the social aspects were less important.

They found that for social tasks, such as getting acquainted or negotiation, interactions were more personalised, less argumentative and more polite when conducted via videomediated communication, that participants believed video-mediated (and face-to-face) communication was superior, and that groups conversing using video-mediated communication tended to like each other more, compared to audio-only interactions. Obviously, some nonverbal communication must be responsible for these differences.

There have been several attempts to develop and evaluate relational agents in HCI research, as well as several commercial products with similar goals. In the commercial arena these products have been mostly toys designed to cultivate a sense of relationship with their users. Most of these artifacts play on people's need to express nurturance by requiring caretaking in order to thrive, or by engaging in familiar social interaction patterns. Many of these artifacts also change their behaviour over time or otherwise provide a highly variable, rich set of expressions to give the sense of uniqueness crucial for relationships.

While some human relational strategies can be implemented in almost any medium, many of the strategies are most effectively conveyed in natural language dialogue, or even require an animated human body to enact. Given that relational agents are those intended to produce a relational response in their users, such as increased liking for or trust in the agent, the studies by Reeves and Nass and their students on relational aspects of human-computer interaction constitute the bulk of work in this area to date. The majority of these studies use non-embodied, textonly human-computer interfaces. Relational Effects Means:

— Computers that use flattery, or which praise rather than criticise their users are better liked.

— Computers that praise other computers are better liked than computers that praise themselves, and computers that criticise other computers are liked less than computers that criticise themselves.

— Users prefer computers that match them in personality over those that do not (the "similarity attraction" principle).

— Users prefer computers that become more like them over time over those which maintain a consistent level of similarity, even when the resultant similarity is the same.

— Users who are "teamed" with a computer will think better of the computer and cooperate more with it than those who are not teamed (the "in-group membership" effect, which can be achieved by simply signifying that the user and computer are part of a team).

Other studies within this computers as social actors paradigm include one by Morkes, Kernal and Nass, who demonstrated that computer agents that use humor are rated as more likable, competent and cooperative than those that do not. Moon also demonstrated that a computer that uses a strategy of reciprocal, deepening self-disclosure in its (text-based) conversation with the user will cause the user to rate it as more attractive, divulge more intimate information, and become more likely to buy a product from the computer.

In a recent attempt to challenge the Media Equation, Shechtman and Horowitz did a study in which participants interacted with a computer system in solving the Desert Survival Problem via a text chat interface, with half of the subjects told they were interacting with a computer and half told they were interacting remotely with another human. They found that participants used significantly more words and spent longer in discussion, and used over four times as much relational language, when they thought they were interacting with another human compared to when they thought they were interacting with a computer.

However, given that subjects were told they were interacting with a computer, that the interface itself did not present any social cues beyond those in the natural language text, and that these text responses apparently included little or no relational language (and no uptake on subject's relational language), their outcome does not say anything about the inclination of people to use relational language with a truly relational agent or their ability to bond with them. Following a long line of research on the impact of mirroring behaviours on social distance.

Evaluated the degree to which a computer character's mirroring a user's intonation patterns affected the user's attitudes towards the character. They demonstrated that the more frequently the computer matched the user in intonation (producing non-linguistic, hummed outputs) the higher the user rated the computer on measures of familiarity, including comfortableness, friendliness, and perceived sympathy.

There has also been a fair amount of work over the last few decades on people's perceptions of trust in man-made artifacts, particularly in machinery and, more recently, computers. Tseng and Fogg define trust as "a positive belief about the perceived reliability of, dependability of, and confidence in a person, object, or process," and claim that it is one of the key components used in assessments of "computer credibility".

Graman-computer interfaces has found several interesting results with respect to trust. It has been found that trust in intelligent systems is higher for systems that can explain and justify their decisions There have also been studies showing how specific design elements, such as the use of colour and clipart or the inclusion of comprehensive product information can influence a user's perception of trust in an interface. In anthropomorphic interfaces, pedagogical agents, especially those that are highly expressive, have been found to affect students' perceptions of trust; such agents are perceived as helpful, believable, and concerned.

SOCIAL DISCOURSE PLANNING

Few systems in the literature have used explicit relational models in an ongoing way, and only one has used such a model for assessing ever-changing relational variables and generating dialogue moves based on these variables: the REA agent. The social dialogue planner developed for the REA system was the first to use an explicit model of the agentuser relationship, which was both dynamically updated and used for dialogue planning during the course of a conversation. The planner was designed to sequence agent utterances-both task and social-in order to satisfy both task and relational constraints.

REA is a real-time, multi-modal, life-sized embodied conversational agent that plays the role of a real estate agent who can interview potential home buyers and show them around virtual houses for sale. Real estate sales was selected as the application domain for REA specifically because of the opportunity it presented to explore a task domain in which a significant amount of relational dialogue normally occurs. Within this domain the initial interview between an agent and a prospective buyer was modeled.

The planner makes contributions to the conversation in order to minimise the threat to the user (e.g., talk about personal finances is more threatening than talk about the weather), while pursuing task goals in the most efficient manner possible. That is, it attempts to determine the threat of the next conversational move, assess the solidarity and familiarity that currently holds with the user, and judge which topics will seem most relevant and least intrusive to users.

As a function of these factors, it chooses whether or not to engage in social dialogue, and what kind of social dialogue to choose. The discourse planner integrates a number of non-discrete factors in an activation network framework in which each of the actions represents a conversational move the agent can make. These factors include: threat to the user (a property of topics, e.g., finance is more threatening than talk about the weather); coherence of the move with the current topic of conversation (based on a measure of similarity between the move's topic and the current topic); and relevance of the move.

A key aspect of relationship is that it is a persistent construct, spanning multiple interactions. Yet, all studies to date on relational agents-and conversational agents in general-have used single-session experimental designs. Further, there already exist brief duration techniques for effecting health behaviour change, many of which have been successfully computerised. Exercise adoption was selected as the target behaviour for the study because it gave participants a motive to interact with the system on a daily basis, given that the current government guidelines are that all adults engage in thirty minutes or more of moderate-intensity physical activity on most, and preferably all, days of the week.

Fit Track System

The MIT Fit Track system was designed to be used by study participants on their home computers on a daily basis during a one-month intervention, with each interaction lasting approximately ten minutes. The intervention coupled state-of-the-art behaviour change techniques with a relational agent who played the role of an exercise advisor that participants talked to about their physical activity.

Major aspects of the system design were based on studies of interactions between professional exercise trainers and clients, surveys of representative study participants, literature reviews of therapist-client and physician-client interactions and health behaviour change methodology. In order to support a large number of study participants on a wide range of personal computers, a client-server architecture was developed in which the client (running on participants' computers) was kept as lightweight as possible.

The client consists of two web browsers coupled with a vector-graphics-based embodied conversational agent synchronised with a text-to-speech engine. All dialogue and application logic, as well as the relational database backend, was kept on the server. Although the agent uses synthesised speech and synchronised nonverbal behaviour, user contributions to the dialogue are made primarily by selecting items from multiplechoice menus of text phrases, dynamically updated based on the conversational context.

Even in the Wizard-Of-Oz setup used in the REA study, in which understanding was performed by a human confederate, subjects found that the agent's fixed repertoire of output utterances left them feeling that REA wasn't really listening to them. More importantly, by constraining what the user can say in every context, the agent's responses can be crafted to cover the entire space of possible inputs.

In addition to network branching operations, ATN actions can include saving values to the database or retrieving and testing values from the database, in order to support the ability to remember things about users and to be able to refer back to prior conversations. For example, it could remember that the user said she liked to exercise with a buddy, and ask her about such opportunities in a future dialogue. Utterances output to the agent could be tailored at runtime through the inclusion of phrases derived from information in the database or other sources (template-based generation).

The embodied agent had a range of non-verbal behaviours that it used for co-verbal communicative and interactional functions, including: hand gestures, body posture shifts, gazing at and away from the user, raising and lowering eyebrows, head nods, and walking on and off the screen. It also supported four different facial expressions, variable proximity and several idle-time behaviours.

Co-verbal behaviour was specified one utterance at a time in XML messages sent from the server to the client. This behaviour was determined for each utterance using the BEAT text-to-embodied-speech system, with several enhancements to support the exercise dialogues.

The model of relationship used by the Fit Track agent is essentially a stage model, in which the trajectory of change in the relationship is fixed over the 30 scripted dialogues. The working alliance is thought to increase to a stable level after approximately seven sessions in psychotherapy, so the relational strategies used by the agent are phased in over the first seven interactions.

10

LEARNING TECHNOLOGY PRACTICES WITH TOOLKITS

Learning technology is an inherently multi-disciplinary field, and stakeholders include of researchers from different fields as well as teaching subject-experts who engage with it as 'end users' or 'consumers'. This multi-disciplinarity is a common feature of emergent research areas and, in one sense, is a strength. However, if we are to capitalise on this richness of expertise, it is necessary to work towards a clear theoretical underpinning that allows these diverse cultures to engage with and develop the use of learning technology. An important starting point for any discussion of this type is the realisation that learning technology use is shaped by contextual factors.

DEVELOPMENT OF STRATEGIES

A range of aids and resources to facilitate decision-making processes has developed to support the use and integration of learning technologies. As a consequence, the terms 'tools', 'toolkits', 'frameworks', 'good practice' and 'model' abound, but are very rarely used with any consistency. Indeed, there is considerable confusion and overlap within the literature on the precise nature of these types of resources.

A number of pedagogic frameworks have been developed to support learning technology. All develop from a particular theoretical viewpoint (whether explicitly or implicitly), aiming to encourage the application of good practice according to a specific pedagogical approach. This provides a structured approach to integrating learning materials into courses. The framework is designed to support the process of 're-engineering' a course.

It provides a framework in which various features of an existing course can be described and evaluated, allowing an analysis of strengths and weaknesses, the suitability of different media types and limiting factors, including resource issues and local constraints. The framework can be applied as a series of stages, working through a process of shortlisting and selection of alternative teaching techniques, and concluding with a mapping of the new course.

Frameworks and wizards, both share a common aim of supporting a users' engagement with an area. Clearly, however, they are working at very different levels and making different assumptions about the type of support that the user might need. Theoretical frameworks provide a structure and vocabulary that support the exploration of concepts and issues. Wizards provide automated processes that support the production or selection of resources, and are predicated on the assumption that the user is primarily concerned with efficiency rather than critical engagement.

Fundamental concerns (for example, about the suitability of using a particular type of resource) are either ignored or assumed by the wizards. These two positions can be characterised as extremes of one continuum. At one extreme there are frameworks, which are flexible and versatile, but which offer relatively little support for practitioners attempting to engage with them.

At the other there are wizards and templates, which are highly restrictive, but (by virtue of the constraints that they impose) are able to offer much closer support and guidance to users.

Between these extremes lie a range of resources, including checklists, guidelines and step-by-step tutorials. Toolkits can be viewed as a mid-point on this continuum: they are decision-making systems based on expert models. A model is taken to be a simplified account of reality that can be used to explain or predict certain features. In toolkits, models tend to be of design processes. Toolkits are more structured than frameworks; they use a model of a design or decision-making process, together with tools provided at key decision-making points, to help the user engage with a theoretical framework and apply it in the context of their own practice.

Each of the tools that is drawn upon as the user works through the process model is designed to help the user to access a knowledge base in order to make informed decisions. The format of toolkits means that they can be used in a standard, linear fashion, or can be "dipped into" by users whose level of expertise is stronger in some areas of the design process than others. Toolkits represent a mid-point between facilitated, uncritical development of resources and a deep engagement with fundamental issues and theories.

They are not intended to replace expertise, although they are intended to reduce the need for prior expertise before practitioners are able to engage with fundamental issues in a meaningful way. As such, they can be viewed as a steppingstone between uncritical and autonomously critical engagement with an area.

It became clear just how closely toolkits were related to expert systems. The close relationship arises from the shared aim of both types of resource to encapsulate methods and theory within a software tool. In addition, it is recognised that both types of resource embodies "claims" about the world that can be reverse-engineered through claims analysis. Toolkits and expert systems differ in four important respects.

Firstly, unlike most expert systems, the emphasis with a toolkit is not on providing answers or knowledge in response to a query. Instead, the focus is on modelling the user's practice. The creation and analysis of these models then forms the basis for the creation of plans, knowledge and understanding that is directly related to the user's context and cultural practices.

Toolkits are designed to address multiple distinct areas of knowledge, and in many ways the "tools" designed for some of these areas could be described as being like expert systems, to the extent that some of them make recommendations based on a representation of an underlying knowledge base.

However, we argue that one important defining feature of toolkits is the relationship between these modular elements - the focus is on the sustained engagement, by the user, in order to draw together a string of such advice, rather than on one output generated by the system and presented to the user.

Another important distinction is that toolkits do not embody a claim to "expertise". Instead, their claims are far more tentative. Rather than attempting to be authoritative or definitive, toolkits are predicated on the basis of utility. Specifically, they are judged on how useful the system of classification used to represent the underlying knowledge base is in terms of supporting decision making.

This represents an important move away from legitimation in terms of meta-narratives and towards a performative definition of value. However, unlike many other forms of commodified knowledge, it is the user, not the designer, who decides on the legitimacy of the representation.

The descriptive systems, the frameworks drawn upon in the toolkit, simply act as a starting point that can be debated, adapted, revised and so on. Thus instead of being expert systems, they might more accurately be called "amateurs" systems. The plurality of that last point leads on to the fourth important distinction between expert systems and toolkits. Toolkits are about each user's domain, rather than one idealised domain.

The framework and knowledge base provide a way of describing what users do in some area of practice - hence the link made to modelling, above. The knowledge base described at each step can, and we argue should, be altered by the user to reflect their own practice. Moreover, toolkits are designed so that each knowledge domain described can be extended, as well as amended, by the users.

The implication of this is that toolkits cannot be expert systems as traditionally understood, although with sustained use, an individual users' adapted instance of a toolkit might conceivably be described as an expert model of their own practice. Essentially, then, we see toolkits as having a new niche in terms of modelling end user expertise. Unlike expert systems, which present themselves as authoritative and definitive, toolkits adopt a more postmodern position on the problems of practice, celebrating difference, contextuality and a democratic form of interaction that allows the user to create and direct instead of being directed.

In this sense, they are perhaps best located as a means of representing and sharing practice, rather than a way of privately receiving advice on one's own practice.

Importantly, this modelling of experience an interative process, which may start from an initial, general given model of the domain. This gives rise to a fifth distinguishing feature of toolkits, which arises as a corollary from the above points: that unlike systems which take a static snapshot of expertise, toolkits evolve.

Epistemology of Toolkits

The distinction between toolkits and other kinds of decision support tools has its roots in a distinctive epistemological position. Whereas expert systems present an authoritative model of a particular realm of knowledge, toolkits are concerned with personal, contextual and often fragmented representations.

a) Theoretical knowledge, such as models, frameworks, and so on. Here, we are concerned with the transformation of these forms of knowledge as 'given', being legitimated by their acceptance within expert communities, into peformative kinds of knowledge (such as a system) that can help guide the user towards particular things that would be of use.

b) The tacit knowledge essential to professional practice. We are interested in making this knowledge explicit. This is achieved by the elicitation of users' own practices as part of their use of the tool. This elicitation may be achieved syntactically; however, at other times, it involves the construction of visual or multimodal representations, echoing the new forms of scholarly discourse and rhetoric discussed by Ingraham.

The latter in particular is novel in the context of decision support tools. Traditionally, most expert systems have been restricted to formalised, well-defined areas of knowledge that can be represented in relatively stable, conventional ways. However, it is in the context of the situated, ill-defined, poorly understood areas of tacit knowledge about professional practice that toolkits demonstrate their value -and this is perhaps their key benefits.

The reason toolkits are so interesting is because they are able to extend the range of existing decision support tools beyond the individual instances of stable knowledge in well defined areas and out into the murky waters of professional practice. This is achieved by putting the provisional nature of models centre-stage, allowing them to be adapted and refined in the light of users' beliefs and local situations, and also by emphasising that users should describe their own (situated) practice rather than attempting to work with an externally-imposed 'ideal' model.

It also emphasises the importance of viewing toolkits as representations to be contested, of drawing the users' attention to their rhetorical and constituting effect, so that they may debate, refine or replace the models that are used to reflect their practices. There are, inevitably, limits on the kinds of knowledge that are appropriate to address toolkits. The kind of codification envisaged thus far concentrates on design and decision making, and we suspect that this may well represent the appropriate scope for tools of this type.

RATIONALE FOR TOOLKITS

In recent years, nationally policy has placed a considerable emphasis on the embedding of new technology into the learning and teaching process. However, the embedding process is not trivial, and uptake has traditionally been patchy. One reason for this is the considerable range of skills that need to be acquired if embedding is to be carried out in a professional way.

Despite the current policies which advocate that adapting and re-using existing learning materials and a more extensive use of learning technologies to support learning and teaching is a good thing, examples of this are few and far between.

This can be traced to a number of factors. In particular, the 'not invented here' syndrome is no doubt still present. However, more important perhaps is the issue of the time and skills required to evaluate and then adapt materials or gain expertise in understanding and utilising learning technologies. The latter is compounded by the fact that finding these materials in the first place is a non-trivial exercise (although the growth of subject-specific information gateways, portals and guidelines to resources will go some way towards alleviating this problem).

Some of the barriers to uptake which have been identified include: the problem of finding relevant materials in the first place, the difficulty of adapting other peoples' materials, the issue of ownership and copyright, integration with other materials, including issues of style, definition and level, staff having the appropriate educational and/or technical skills required to evaluate, adapt and integrate materials, and concern about the currency of materials, particularly accuracy and whether it is up-to-date.

Equally significant is the problem that large amounts of research and theory on the use of such resources remains unfamiliar to practitioners. Whilst it would be unreasonable to expect subject specialists to dedicate themselves to the study of and engagement with this area, problems can arise when these people begin to adopt learning technology.

In such situations, it is important to consider how these practitioners can best be supported, and whether that support should focus on addressing basic needs (such as efficient production, suggesting the need for tools such as wizards) or should encourage them to engage at a deeper level. The continuum of support outlined earlier suggests that one solution to this problem may be to provide a series of steps, through which support is steadily phased out whilst flexibility and versatility is introduced.

Toolkits are intended to act as a mid-point in this transitional process, allowing greater engagement than wizards and templates can, but providing more structure and support than a theoretical framework. Another important feature of toolkits concerns the decision-making activities that the user can engage with whilst following the expert model. As noted, these are intended to support the user in the process of making informed decisions; they rely on a structured description of a relevant knowledge base that can be automatically searched (based on information elicited from the user) in order to suggest approaches that might be relevant.

By layering progressively more detailed information on the options available, the user is able to follow up when and if this is required. For example, if presented with a shortlist of suggested methods, a user might immediately be able to reject familiar and unsuitable options simply from their title. Unfamiliar options might require short explanatory or illustrative information before they could be accepted or rejected, and some might warrant detailed discussions (perhaps including illustrative case studies). Because this simple layered structure presents information 'on demand', rather than expecting the user to wade through tracts of material that may or may not be relevant, they are quicker and easier to use than handbooks, cookbooks or other traditional sources of advice and guidance.

The implication of this is that toolkits should help to reduce the time required in planning work of this type. The aspiration is that toolkits can be used iteratively, with progressively more detailed analysis occurring once initial feedback about the viability of the initial design has been received. In summary, toolkits are predicated on the assumptions that they will be:

— Derived from an explicit theoretical framework.

— Easy-to-use for practitioners.

— Able to provide demonstrable benefit.

— Able to provide guidance, without being prescriptive.

— Adaptable to reflect the user's practice and beliefs.

— Able to produce outputs that reflect the local context.

EVALUATION OF TOOLKITS

The process of the development of each toolkit consists of a number of steps, which are can be coached in terms of framing questions. All three of the toolkits outlined below fit this criterion. Learning technologies have impacted significantly in the areas of curriculum design, evaluation and information handling. Their introduction has added a degree of complication and new forms of expertise to the extent that practitioners need support and guidance, which is a fundamental component of the toolkits. With respect to curriculum design, for example, key issues for practitioners include making sense of the range of learning technologies which can be used to support learning and teaching receiving guidance on how to integrate these effectively with traditional tools and techniques.

A lack of understanding of the precise impact of learning technologies, a better knowledge of their strengths and weaknesses, and some understanding of potential costs and benefits, are some of the evaluation topics which practitioners now need to address. In terms of information handling, the shear enormity of scale of the resources and information available now, along with the increasingly sophisticated online information tools, gateways and portals, means that practitioners also now need some guidance on and understanding of how to utilise this.

Theoretical underpinning: This step makes explicit the underlying theory and expert model to be used by the toolkit, providing a frame of reference and an initial structure for decision making.

Toolkit specification: How can the range of options available at each stage be translated into a practical but flexible form of guidance for non-experts? A rough outline of the toolkit is drawn-up, based on the framework, which will include the description and structuring of the options (knowledge base) open to users at each decision making step. The toolkits are designed to be easy-to-use, with information structured in layers of increasingly detailed material so as to support flexible use, allowing users to bypass sections with little or no relevance to them or engage deeply with content that they find important.

Toolkit refinement: At this stage, a prototype of the toolkit is tested with end users and evaluated to assess its suitability, ease of use, flexibility and relevance. Feedback from this formative evaluation stage is used to highlight which aspects of the toolkit the users find most useful, and whether there are any important steps or resources omitted. This information is used to iteratively improve the toolkit and provide a more detailed specification. Considerable attention is given to the users' needs, particularly how easy the toolkit is to use and how valuable and useful it is perceived to be. User trials also aim to demonstrate that the toolkit is usable without the support of expert guidance, which represents an important part of the initial assumptions behind the development of toolkits.

Inclusion of user defined features: User trials also assess the flexibility of the toolkit to take account of adaptation by end users. Identification of common adaptations, which are likely to be of wider value, can be incorporated into the core functionality of the toolkit at this stage.

Building shared resources: Use of each toolkit produces some form of 'plan' for a particular task; for example an evaluation strategy to assess a range of web resources, an outline for a new curriculum with a map of learning and teaching tools and techniques, or an information plan for resources for a research project. The user can keep this private, perhaps iteratively refining it over time based on experience or developing understandings. However there are potentially a number of additional uses for the plan.

It could be used as one of a suite of shared resources, for example a set of curriculum plans for a whole course, evaluation strategies for commonly encountered evaluation studies, or information resources to support a consortium-based research. This is a valuable additional aspect of the toolkits and provides a means of addressing some of issues about re-purposing materials and sharing skills sets outlined by Phelps et al. and Beetham.

Illustrative Toolkits

Key findings from the formative evaluations of these toolkits will be summarised and perceived benefits identified.

A toolkit for curriculum design: Media Adviser is a toolkit that can support practitioners redesigning curricula and, in particular, helps them to consider how to appropriately integrated learning technologies alongside more traditional learning and teaching methods. It derives from a broader conceptual pedagogical framework for integrating learning technologies into courses that maps out and compares traditional modes of delivery with learning technologies.

It considers different learning and teaching methods in terms of their relevance and value against a set of four types of teaching activity, namely - delivery, discussion, activity and feedback. These four activities were adapted from the more descriptive set of twelve interactions described in Laurillard's conversational model, and are intended to reflect the values of the socio-constructivist tradition that she draws upon.

In addition to its role in providing support for curriculum re-design, the toolkit has been used successfully to engage practitioners in discussions about their own context and practice - for example, by encouraging a group of practitioners to debate the relevance and meaning of the four 'types' of teaching activity, whether or not refinements or adaptations of this set are warranted, and how these activities might be perceived by learners.

This was the first toolkit developed using the methodology outlined above. As the explanation below illustrates, the formative evaluation of an initial prototype combined with a process of iterative tailoring to meet users' needs is an important feature of this approach. The evaluation also generated a number of unexpected results. In particular, mapping teaching techniques in terms of their support for the four 'types' described above was originally intended as a way of identifying aspects of learning that were systematically emphasised or neglected in a course.

However, evaluation showed this was at least as important as a way for individuals to express their own approach to teaching, or to develop ideas about new ways in which traditional resources could be incorporated into the course. Moreover, the simplicity of the description meant that it could be used as the starting point for comparisons or discussions between practitioners about the differences in their approach to teaching.

What was important with this toolkit was that it raised awareness of the potential uses of learning technologies, in particular in terms of educational value, and therefore formed a good starting point in terms of considering the role of these resources within a particular course. The toolkit was then used to aggregate these individual descriptions of techniques in order to form a more holistic course structure. Media Adviser provides a mechanism to help lecturers think about the different tools and techniques they could use in their teaching and most importantly how these could be considered under the four broad educational activities.

The Evaluation Toolkit provides a structured resource to help practitioners evaluate a range of learning resources and activities. It guides them through the scoping, planning, implementation, analysis and reporting of an evaluation. It assists the practitioner in designing progressively more detailed evaluations, and allows users to access and share evaluation case studies.

It consists of three sections: Planner, Adviser and Presenter, which guide the user through the evaluation process; from the initial scoping of the evaluation question(s) and associated stakeholders, through selection of data capture and analysis methods, and finally through the presentation of the findings. One of the emerging benefits of this toolkit is that the plan the user produces can be made available to other as a case study or example for particular types of evaluation.

Information Processing

The information toolkit adopts a similar approach to Media Adviser and the Evaluation Toolkit. It provides a means of mapping information resources against types of information activity (defined in the toolkit as gathering, processing, communicating and evaluating). This helps the user to gain an understanding of the resources they are using and what they are using them for, to help them produce their own tailored information plan. The toolkit guides the user through the process of articulating their information needs and results in the production of an information plan for a particular task.

The 'scope' of the task is one of the first stages of working through the toolkit; a task could involve considering all the information needs of a course team developing a course module. As with both Media Adviser and the Evaluation Toolkit, this can be used to build shared information plans in the form of case studies or templates. It is suitable for use across a range of levels of expertise and valuable for both learners and researchers.

The evaluation of the toolkits was designed to provide feedback on the usability of toolkits and to assess their potential impact on practice. The methodology used includes observational studies and a follow up workshop with new users. In the initial stage, usability trials in the form of cognitive walkthroughs are carried out. These are used to improve the design and layout of a toolkit and to help the content developers to identify areas that required further work and improvement.

In each case a researcher observes and records the user's activities. At the end of a session users also provide feedback on the overall use and value of a toolkit, areas for improvement, and whether format of a toolkit had influenced the way in which they had approached their planning process. Feedback from these trials is used to improve the toolkits and in particular the overall structure and navigation of the resources. Once an updated version of a toolkit had been produced, taking into account all the feedback from the initial usability trails, the second phase of the evaluation is carried out.

This takes the form of one or more workshops comprising a range of potential users. They are asked to keep a record of their activities and in particular to note any reflections as well as any benefits or problems encountered. At appropriate points the group is drawn together to discuss progress and in particular good and bad features of the toolkit. Early feedback on the toolkits in these evaluation stages tends to concentrate on usability issues and navigation.

Users are often frustrated by the early navigational structure and layout of the toolkits, which can fundamentally impede their progress and hamper their understanding of the issues and concepts being described. In each case, the toolkit is refined in light of such comments, with the result that the usability is markedly improved by the end of the project.

Feedback on the content and potential usefulness of the toolkits has generally been positive. Users clearly benefit from working through them and recognised that they were rich resources of material. However, there was some concern that the Evaluation Toolkit was deceptive in terms of its size and ease of use. In general it was recommended that users should be made more clearly aware of the time required to complete each toolkit and the level of detail and concentration required if the user were to gain optimal value from using the resources.

It was encouraging to note that the improvements made to the toolkit as the result of initial feedback are noticeable in the way that the workshop users work through the resources much more easily. Reassuringly, however, the toolkit was able to support complete novices. The emphasis on 'contexts' and reasons for evaluation throughout the toolkit is very helpful, because there is perhaps a tendency to report what was done on a particular project rather than actually evaluating that project and how useful its outcomes are to the stakeholders.

The toolkit seems to bring the user back to this point all the time - which would be very helpful, particularly in a big project, or one with lots of interested parties. There were, however, some limits on willingness to engage with such theoretical positions. For example, the evaluation toolkit is designed to recommend particular methods for data collection and analysis based on the question asked. This is achieved by filtering the methods using the (editable) representations of the knowledge base on data collection and analysis methods.

Media Adviser

A small-scale study with Media Adviser was carried out that involved three users, two drawn from one course team and one drawn from a different faculty. Each had experience of teaching on a number of courses, but had chosen one course that they felt needed changing. The jointly-taught course was a first-year unit in a medical programme, taken by around 120 students, roughly three quarters of whom were taking the course as part of a subsidiary subject.

It is taken by around twenty students, half from within the economics department, and half from the faculty of social sciences. This mix allowed differences in practice both within and between faculties to be illustrated. The workshop was run by one facilitator, with an additional observer taking notes and helping out when required. Even from the first activity - which simply involved listing the teaching methods used during the course - participants started to reflect on fundamental issues of course design, such as the difference between a teacher-centred and a student-centred description of the course.

As with the Evaluation Toolkit, engagement with the software led the lecturers to challenge their previously taken-for-granted course design practices, which they came to realise reflected tradition rather than any explicit theory of learning. The second activity, which involved using the rater tool to describe their teaching, led to further questioning of the role of different educational techniques. This led to a rich discussion of student expectations and institutional policies, raising participants' awareness of the marketing and political aspects of course design.

It also highlighted the way in which familiar formats can appear to be engaging without actually involving the student in anything more than a passive, receptive role. Students seem to want to feel that they have participated, and somehow, by sitting through a lecture, they think they have done. The descriptive process also highlighted differences in teaching style. For example, one participant characterised their lectures as involving a high degree of activity and discussion for students; this contrasted with the two lecturers who both taught as part of one course team, for whom lectures were primarily a means of disseminating information to students. Similarly, all three had differing views about what constituted a tutorial.

Importantly, there were differences between the two members of the course team that had not previously been recognised. This led to a discussion of how each participant ran their tutorials, and an exchange of suggestions about how they could be made more interactive and engaging. As one participant noted, such discussions provided obvious opportunities to extend lecturers' repertoire of techniques by learning about "the different ways in which people use handouts, tutorials, lectures, etc." The result of this was the early sharing of plans for change that were grounded in participants' own experiences.

As part of these discussions, the participants began to identify reasons why teaching techniques such as lectures differed. 'Disciplinary differences' were initially cited as one possible reason, but the existence of differences within the course team led to a more critical discussion of what this phrase might actually mean. Eventually, a number of influences were identified, each of which contributed to the process of determining the format of teaching, including.

In recognition of these influences, the participants recognised that there would never be agreement as to the 'right' way to describe a lecture, tutorial, etc. However, they felt that descriptions of techniques would "start off differently, but might converge" as users of the toolkit debated their understanding of the descriptive language and reached consensus over the meanings of terms. In a similar vein, the participants discussed whether or not to introduce less familiar techniques, such as web-based teaching, computer-mediated communication, and so on.

Importantly, there was valuable discussion about what these terms meant to the participants, and what role they might have in teaching and learning. This clarification enabled him to plan changes to his course in greater detail, concentrating on pedagogic requirements rather than the technical systems available to him.

11

CONSTRUCTIVE ONLINE LEARNING

Constructivism is a theory of learning that has roots in both philosophy and psychology. The essential core of constructivism is that learners actively construct their own knowledge and meaning from their experiences. This core has roots that extend back through many years and many philosophers. Philosophically, this essence relies on an epistemology that stresses subjectivism and relativism, the concept that while reality may exist separate from experience, it can only be known through experience, resulting in a personally unique reality. There are proposed three essential epistemological tenets of constructivism to which a fourth has been added in light of recent writings.

— Knowledge is not passively accumulated, but rather, is the result of active cognising by the individual;

— Cognition is an adaptive process that functions to make an individual's behavior more viable given a particular environment;

— Cognition organises and makes sense of one's experience, and is not a process to render an accurate representation of reality; and

— Knowing has roots in both biological/neurological construction, and social, cultural, and language based interactions.

Thus, constructivism acknowledges the learner's active role in the personal creation of knowledge, the importance of experience (both individual and social) in this knowledge creation process, and the realisation that the knowledge created will vary in its degree of validity as an accurate representation of reality. These four fundamental tenets provide the foundation for basic principles of the teaching, learning, and knowing process as described by constructivism. As will be seen, however, these tenets may be emphasised differently, resulting in various "degrees" or "types" of constructivism.

CATEGORIES OF CONSTRUCTIVISM

Constructivism is not a unitary theoretical position; rather, it is a continuum. The assumptions that underlie this continuum vary along several dimensions and have resulted in the definition and support for multiple types of constructivism. Typically, this continuum is divided into three broad categories: (a) *cognitive constructivism,* (b) *social constructivism,* and (c) *radical constructivism.*

Cognitive Constructivism

Cognitive constructivism represents one end, or extreme, of the constructivist continuum and is typically associated with information processing and its reliance on the component processes of cognition. While emerging from the four, previously mentioned, epistemological tenets, cognitive constructivism only emphasises the first two tenets, that is, that knowledge acquisition is an adaptive process and results from active cognising by the individual learner. These particular epistemological emphases lead to defining principles that maintain the external nature of knowledge and the belief that an independent reality exists and is knowable to the individual.

Knowledge then, from the cognitive constructivist position, is the result of the accurate internalisation and (re)construction of external reality. The results of this internalisation process are cognitive processes and structures that accurately correspond to processes and structures that exist in the real world. This claim, that reality is knowable to the individual, differentiates cognitive constructivism from both social and radical constructivism.

This process of internalisation and reconstruction of external reality is learning. That is, learning is the process of building accurate internal models or representations that mirror or reflect external structures that exist in the "real" world. This perspective on learning focuses on

a) The procedures or processes of learning,
b) How what is learned is represented or symbolised in the mind, and
c) How these representations are organised within the mind.

Cognitive constructivism, as a learning theory, is often considered a "weak" form of constructivism, within the constructivist community, since it only embraces two of the four epistemological tenets. "Weak" in this case is not a value judgement, such as better or worse, but rather merely an indication of adherence to foundational assumptions. Thus , knowledge construction is considered primarily a technical process of creating mental structures, but has little bearing on the nature of the subjective knowledge within the mind. However, cognitive constructivism, and its historical association with information processing, has led to a multitude of significant empirical findings regarding learning, memory, and cognition, including schema theory, working memory models, computational models of learning and memory, and neurological models of brain function.

In addition, each of these theoretical advances has led to successful instructional applications, such as the use of advanced organisers, concept maps, teaching for transfer, elaborative practice, teaching for automaticity, and the use reading strategies and problem solving strategies (e.g., IDEAL; Identify problems, Define goals, Explore strategies, Act, Learn). Thus, while the cognitive constructivist perspective has proved to be quite beneficial to the understanding of learning and instruction, it remains the "black sheep" of the constructivist community since its focus does not include the subjective nature of knowledge.

Radical Constructivism

Radical constructivism represents the opposite end of the constructivist continuum from cognitive constructivism. Radical constructivism fully embraces the first three epistemological tenets, that is, that knowledge acquisition is an adaptive process that results from active cognising by the individual learner, rendering an experientially based mind, not a mind that reflects some external reality. In addition, there is a current movement within radical constructivism to more fully accept the fourth epistemological tenet, thus recognising social interactions as a source of knowledge. These particular epistemological emphases leads to defining principles that maintain the internal nature of knowledge and the idea that while an external reality may exist, it is unknowable to the individual.

Reality is unknowable since our experience with external forms is mediated by our senses, and our senses are not adept at rendering an accurate representation of these external forms (e.g., objects, social interactions). Therefore, while knowledge is constructed from experience, that which is constructed is not, in any discernible way, an accurate representation of the external world or reality. The adaptive nature of knowledge underscores that knowledge is not objective "truth," that is, internal knowledge does not match external reality, but rather is a viable model of experience. These viable models are created within an individual, influenced by the context within which an activity was experienced, and relative to the accomplishment of a particular goal.

Knowledge is knowledge of the knower, not knowledge of the external world; improving knowledge means improving its viability or fit in, but not match with, an external world. An evaluation of radical constructivism results in radical constructivism being considered a "strong" form of constructivism, as it fully embraces three of the constructivist epistemological tenets and at least partially embraces the fourth. That is, radical constructivism is concerned with both the construction of mental structures, the position of cognitive constructivists, and the construction of personal meaning. In this sense, radical constructivism involves a greater degree of construction than does cognitive constructivism, involving two planes of construction, structure and meaning, rather than only one, structure.

Social Constructivism

Social constructivism lies somewhere between the transmission of knowable reality of the cognitive constructivists, and the construction of a personal and coherent reality of the radical constructivists. Social constructivism, unlike cognitive and radical constructivism, emphasises all four of the previously mentioned epistemological tenets. These particular epistemological emphases lead to defining principles that maintain the social nature of knowledge, and the belief that knowledge is the result of social interaction and language usage, and thus is a shared, rather than an individual, experience.

In addition, this social interaction always occurs within a socio-cultural context, resulting in knowledge that is bound to a specific time and place. This position is exemplifies as "truth is not to be found inside the head of an individual person, it is born between people collectively searching for truth, in the process of their dialogic interaction". Truth, in this case, is neither the objective reality of the cognitive constructivists nor the experiential reality of the radical constructivist, but rather is a socially constructed and agreed upon truth resulting from "co-participation in cultural practices".

Like radical constructivism, social constructivism would be considered a "strong" form of constructivism, emphasising all four of the epistemological tenets. However, social constructivists generally downplay the mental construction of knowledge (not because social constructivists do not believe in mental construction but because it is seen as relatively trivial) and emphasise the co-construction of meaning within a social activity. In this sense, social constructivism is more concerned with meaning than structure.

CONSTRUCTIVIST PEDAGOGY

Constructivist pedagogy, the link between theory and practice, suffers from the breadth of its theoretical underpinnings. Many theorists and practitioners have generated constructivist pedagogies with an array of results. While these pedagogies share a set of core design principles, the peripheral principles tend to vary greatly. The general theoretical and practical constructivist consensus, however, across all three types of constructivism, indicates that eight factors are essential in constructivist pedagogy. It should be noted, though, before the discussion of these principles begins, that these principles are not solely constructivist in nature. Indeed, all of these principles have been proposed by other theories/theorists in other times. What makes this list "constructivist" is the assemblage of these specific principles and the basis/rationale for their inclusion.

— Learning should take place in authentic and real-world environments. Whether building accurate representations of reality, consensual meanings in social activities, or personally coherent models of reality, experience is paramount. Experience, both socially oriented and object oriented, is a primary catalyst of knowledge construction. Experience provides the activity upon which the mind operates. In addition, knowledge construction is enhanced when the experience is authentic. For the cognitive constructivist, authentic experiences are essential so that the individual can construct an accurate representation of the "real" world, not a contrived world. For the social and radical constructivists, authentic experiences are important so that the individual may construct mental structures that are viable in meaningful situations.

— Learning should involve social negotiation and mediation. While only social constructivism emphasises social interaction as a basis for knowledge construction, cognitive and radical constructivisms do assign social interaction a role. Social interaction provides for the development of socially relevant skills and knowledge, as well as providing a mechanism for perturbations that may require individual adaptation. In some cases, such as cultural mores and culturally arbitrary rituals (e.g., greetings, gender relations, dress), knowledge can only be attained through social contact.

In addition, as an individual gains experience in a social situation, this experience may verify an individual's knowledge structures or it may contradict those structures. If there is contradiction or confusion, then the individual must accommodate this contradiction in order to maintain either an accurate model of reality or a coherent personal or social model of reality. Finally, an integral component of social mediation is the use of language. Language is the medium through which knowledge and understanding are constructed in social situations.

— Content and skills should be made relevant to the learner. All three types of constructivism emphasise the concept that knowledge serves an adaptive function. If knowledge is to enhance one's adaptation and functioning, then the knowledge attained must be relevant to the individual's current situation, understanding, and goal. This relevancy is likely to lead to an increase in motivation as the individual comes to understand the need for certain knowledge. Ultimately, experience with relevant tasks will provide the individual with the mental processes, social information, and personal experiences necessary for enhanced functioning within one's practical environment.

— Content and skills should be understood within the framework of the learner's prior knowledge. All learning begins within an individual's prior knowledge, regardless of constructivist affiliation. Understanding a student's behaviour requires an understanding of the student's mental structures, that is, an understanding of the student's understanding. When a student replies that the answer to 54 - 38 is 24, the teacher must not think "Oh, that is wrong," but rather "What is the student's understanding of subtraction that has led to this answer?" In this case, the student appears to be using the following rule of subtraction, "subtract the smallest from the largest." While this rule is "incorrect" given our current system of mathematics, it is, nonetheless, the rule the student is using. Understanding the student's rule usage makes it much easier for the teacher to demonstrate, using manipulatives of some type, the non-viability of the student's understanding. Only by attempting to understand a student's prior knowledge will the teacher be able to create effective experiences, resulting in maximal learning.

— Students should be assessed formatively, serving to inform future learning experiences. Cognitive, social, and radical constructivism all assert that the acquisition of knowledge and understanding is an ongoing process that is heavily influenced by a student's prior knowledge. Unfortunately, knowledge and understanding are not directly visible, but rather must be inferred from action. Thus, to take into account an individual's current level of understanding in this ongoing teaching and learning process, a teacher must continually assess the individual's knowledge. This formative assessment is necessary to accurately create the next series of experiences and activities for students.

— Students should be encouraged to become self-regulatory, self-mediated, and self-aware. The underlying tenet of constructivism, and the main thread that holds together this array of theoretical positions, is the claim that learners are active in their construction of knowledge and meaning. This activity involves mental manipulation and self-organisation of experience, and requires that students regulate their own cognitive functions, mediate new meanings from existing knowledge, and form an awareness of current knowledge structures. Within a cognitive constructivist perspective, self-regulation, self-mediation, and self-awareness would be subsumed under the construct of metacognition. Metacognition is considered an essential aspect of learning and consists of

a) knowledge of cognition (i.e., knowing what one knows, knowing what one is capable of doing, and knowing what to do and when to do it) and

b) regulation of cognition (i.e., the on-going task of planning, monitoring, and evaluating one's own learning and cognition).

While cognitive constructivism would emphasise self-regulation and self-awareness, social and radical constructivism would emphasise self-mediation. Self-mediation is represented within social and radical constructivism by Vygotsky's concept of the psychological tool, and Piaget's concept of reflective abstraction, respectively. Vygotsky believed that students construct mental signs, or psychological tools, to represent concepts and relationships, and that these tools are used to mediate "inter-mental" cognition. Similarly, Piaget theorised that students mentally reflect on the use and nature of objects and then construct new knowledge by generalising, or abstracting, new relationships. The importance of the thought and self-regulation relationship was expressed by Vygotsky, "The system of signs restructures the whole psychological process and enables the child to master her movement".

— Teachers serve primarily as guides and facilitators of learning, not instructors. The role of the teacher in the learning process has often been a major factor in the apparent division between cognitive constructivism and social/radical constructivism. Teachers, in the cognitive constructivist perspective, are usually portrayed as instructors who transmit knowledge. The teacher instructs, while the learner learns. In actuality, in the cognitive constructivist perspective, the role of the teacher is to create experiences in which the students will participate that will lead to appropriate processing and knowledge acquisition.

Consequently, cognitive constructivism supports the teacher as a guide or facilitator to the extent that the teacher is guiding or facilitating relevant processing. Contrarily, since social and radical constructivism eschew any direct knowledge of reality, there is no factual knowledge to transmit and the only role for the teacher is to guide students to an awareness of their experiences and socially agreed-upon meanings. This teacher as guide metaphor indicates that the teacher is to motivate, provide examples, discuss, facilitate, support, and challenge, but not to attempt to act as a knowledge conduit.

— Teachers should provide for and encourage multiple perspectives and representations of content. The relationship of multiple perspectives and multiple representations is one of cause and effect within cognitive constructivism. Experiencing multiple perspectives of a particular event provides the student with the raw materials necessary to develop multiple representations. These multiple representations provide students with various routes from which to retrieve knowledge and the ability to develop more complex schemas relevant to the experience. In addition, in social and radical constructivism there is no privileged "truth," only perceptual understandings that may prove to be more or less viable. This being the case, a student's understanding and adaptability is increased when he or she is able to examine an experience from multiple perspectives. These perspectives provide the student with a greater opportunity to develop a more viable model of their experiences and social interactions.

CONSTRUCTIVISM ONLINE

It needs to be re-emphasised that constructivism is a theory of knowledge acquisition, not a theory of pedagogy; thus, the nexus of constructivism and online education is tentative, at best. Constructivism posits that knowledge acquisition occurs amid four assumptions:

a) Learning involves active cognitive processing.

b) Learning is adaptive.

c) Learning is subjective, not objective.

d) Learning involves both social/cultural and individual processes.

These four assumptions have led, indirectly, to eight primary pedagogical recommendations:

- — Learning should take place in authentic and real-world environments.
- — Learning should involve social negotiation and mediation.
- — Content and skills should be made relevant to the learner.

— Content and skills should be understood within the framework of the learner's prior knowledge.

— Students should be assessed formatively, serving to inform future learning experiences.

— Students should be encouraged to become self-regulatory, self-mediated, and self-aware.

— Teachers serve primarily as guides and facilitators of learning, not instructors.

— Teachers should provide for and encourage multiple perspectives and representations of content.

The question then arises, can an online medium support this pedagogy that is based on the constructivist assumptions. Below, each of the eight pedagogical statements is briefly addressed based on this question and a "grade" is given to reflect online education's ability to meet or implement these statements.

— Learning should take place in authentic and real-world environments. If authenticity were examined as an either/or proposition, then online education would fail miserably; however, authenticity is more a matter of degree than constitution. From this perspective, online education is potentially quite effective in providing virtual environments in which one can simulate real-world events. In order for online education to adequately satisfy this pedagogical statement the online environment must provide complex, culturally relevant, illstructured domains within which the user can operate and "live." The use of virtual reality, simulators, and microworlds has focused on this concept.

— Learning should involve social negotiation and mediation. Online education provides a unique opportunity for students to engage in social negotiation and mediation; unfortunately, until recently, social negotiation and mediation were constrained in the online medium. The use of both asynchronous (e.g., email, threaded discussions, listservs) and synchronous (e.g., MOOs, MUDs, IRCs, video teleconferencing) online communications allows for social negotiation and mediation to occur across both time and distance.

— Content and skills should be made relevant to the learner. Online education is capable of making vast amounts of very diverse information, knowledge, and skills available to the learner. In this sense, online education is quite capable of providing relevance as long as the learner is able to self-select a relevant topic, process, or skill. Where online education may have difficulty is in spontaneously adapting instruction to a change in student perspective. In a face-to-face meeting, when a student asks a question such as "How does this concept relate to my interest?" the teacher is able to adjusting the next response to the clearly fit the student's query; however, most online education interfaces are not flexible enough to handle this type of tailoring. This type of immediate tailoring is more available through synchronous than asynchronous environments.

— Content and skills should be understood within the framework of the learner's prior knowledge. This pedagogical statement is perhaps the most difficult for online education to handle. To address this statement requires a transaction to occur between the user and the online educational environment. In a synchronous environment mediated by an instructor, student's prior knowledge may be probed at the beginning of instruction and instruction may then be adjusted based on the feedback from the student; however, in an asynchronous environment, this type of probing and responding is less fiuid and flexible.

— Students should be assessed formatively, serving to inform future learning experiences. While online environments are capable of frequently assessing students during instruction, difficulty arises in using this formative assessment to guide further instruction. The reason for assessing students formatively is to make adjustments to instruction that take into account the student's currently level of understanding. Instructors will often provide students with "self-check" quizzes that assess students during various parts of instruction; however, the use of these quizzes is usually marginal, providing feedback to students so that students have a better understanding of their learning. Rarely is this knowledge used to alter subsequent instruction.

— Students should be encouraged to become self-regulatory, self-mediated, and selfaware. In most online education environments, self-regulation, self-mediation, and selfawareness are requirements for successfully engaging in that environment. Online education typically requires students to be more involved and more persistent relative to the educational environment. One aspect of online education that is currently lacking is educating the student in the processes necessary to successfully engage in online education. Students often begin an online educational experience with no instruction concerning how online education differs from tradition classroom education. This pedagogical statement is attainable, but is currently not being addressed adequately.

— Teachers serve primarily as guides and facilitators of learning, not instructors. While it is still possible for instructors to lecture and to use direct instruction during an online educational experience, it is not nearly as easy as it is when one is teaching in a classroom. As a result, one is likely to find less "instructing" and more guiding and facilitating in online education. In addition, online education can be effectively constructed to emphasise a facilitating role for instructors while students engage in simulations, web-based data collection, and ill-structured problem solving. The self-regulatory and self-mediated nature of online education promotes the instructor taking the role of guide or coach.

— Teachers should provide for and encourage multiple perspectives and representations of content. Online education, especially with a diverse group of students, is ripe for the presentation and experience of multiple perspectives. Online education has easy access to international and culturally diverse resources, including diverse populations. With the passing of time, a greater amount of diverse articles (published and pre-published) and presentations are accessible online, providing students with the resources for multiple perspectives.

12

VISUAL LITERACY IN LEARNING

Visual literacy is the ability to 'read,' interpret, and understand information presented in pictorial or graphic images. Associated with visual literacy is visual thinking, described as the ability to turn information of all types into pictures, graphics, or forms that help communicate the information.

The presence of visual elements in today's teaching and learning is increasing as the integration of images and visual presentations with text in textbooks, instructional manuals, classroom presentations, and computer interfaces broadens. Although the educational community is embracing visual enhancements in instruction, the connection of visual and verbal information is evident throughout history. According to the poet Simonides, "Words are the images of things"; similarly, Aristotle stated that, "without image, thinking is impossible".

Characters in alphabets began as pictures with meaning. These symbols portray a man-made language with no distinction between words and pictures, just as musical notes convey the language of music. Only after the printing press was invented were illustrations and type separated, with illustrations often falling by the wayside. Recent history shows a reversal in this separation with greater reliance on visually oriented approaches to information presentation. The results are leading to a visualisation movement in modern computing whereby complex computations are presented graphically, allowing for deeper insights as well as heightened abilities to communicate data and concepts.

Visualisation helps make sense of data that may have seemed previously unintelligible. Leonardo da Vinci, in recognising the impossibility of recording volumes of data, translated words into drawings from different aspects. As history repeats itself, we may find that a great deal of information is better presented visually rather than verbally. A culture's predominant mode of literacy depends on the technology and mass media it embraces. In education's continuing mission of meeting the needs of learners, an apparent shift from the long-standing process of reading, writing, counting, and text memorisation skills that may have been appropriate for the medieval clerk, are giving way to skills of analysis and innovation that are considered desirable in today's modern cultures.

Proficiency with words and numbers is insufficient and must be supplemented with additional basic skills as new and emerging technologies permeate activities of daily living. Viewing change with fear and skepticism often accompanies shifts such as these that can revolutionise society. Even Socrates portrayed the new technology of the written word as dangerous and destructive, artificial and rigid, and unresponsive and insensitive. As more visual elements are incorporated to achieve an optimal balance between verbal and visual cues in education, interdependence between the two modes of thought will be fostered. Multiple literacies are necessary to meet the challenges of today's society, literacies that include print literacy, visual literacy, aural literacy, media literacy, computer literacy, cultural literacy, social literacy, and ecoliteracy.

Learning through orderly, sequential, verbal-mathematical, left-hemisphere tasks is a pattern seen frequently in education. Those whose thought processes are predominantly in the right-hemisphere where visual-spatial and nonverbal cognition activities rule frequently may have difficulty capitalising on a learning style that is not compatible with their abilities. Cognitive/learning style defined as "the individual's consistent and characteristic predispositions of perceiving, remembering, organising, processing, thinking, and problem solving" and note that cognitive/learning style is an important factor in individual student differences. Instructional materials as well as teaching styles should be matched with cognitive styles for greatest learner benefits. However, the extent to which individuals are polarised in their brain's abilities to deal with verbal and visual modes of thought is not fully understood, although it is rare for individuals to deal equally effectively in both modes (West).

Most people have a tendency to think in words rather than in pictures, yet the use of visualisation in thinking appears to be increasing. Most visualisation skills can be developed by practice. Even so, students with limited domain knowledge may regard graphics as excess complexities and incomprehensible information if the connections with the concepts are not obvious to them. An additional variation in learners is present in those who may have difficulty with comprehending the spoken or written language, particularly those with language barriers, learning disabilities, and hearing disorders.

If visual literacy is regarded as a language, then there is a need to know how to communicate using this language, which includes being alert to visual messages and critically reading or viewing images as the language of the messages. Visual literacy, like language literacy, is culturally specific although there are universal symbols or visual images that are globally understood.

VISUAL LITERACY AND INSTRUCTIONAL TECHNOLOGY

Branton links visual literacy with constructivist learning through the role of each in acquiring knowledge in the information age. Eric Definition of constructivism learning as a "viewpoint in learning theory which holds that individuals acquire knowledge by building it from innate capabilities interacting with the environment" are merged by Branton as explores the possibility that the visual arts taught in a constructivist learning environment can enhance visual literacy skills.

Technology, particularly the graphical user interface of the World Wide Web, requires skills for reading and writing visually in order to derive meaning from what is being communicated. Two major approaches have been suggested for developing visual literacy skills. The first is to help learners read or decode visuals through practicing analysis techniques. Decoding involves interpreting and creating meaning from visual stimuli. The second is to help learners write or encode visuals as a tool for communication. Students develop their visual abilities through use. Sinatra compares the creation of visual messages to writing word messages, in that visual messages have a combination of objects, space, light, angle, and mood to suggest a particular message or effect just as the writer uses words, sentences, and paragraphs to achieve a particular style.

The use of visual literacy ideas and strategies to enhance verbal learning is important. Because visual literacy precedes verbal literacy in human development, it is the basic literacy in the thought processes that are the foundations for reading and writing. "Seeing comes before words. The child looks and recognises before it can speak". Action activities provide the concrete base for the abstract use of symbols in defining and explaining the action activities. These activities of action progress to activities of observation which then are followed by abstract representations, a process that facilitates reconceptualisation and understanding of the experience before describing it verbally. Because pictures or illustrations are analogs of experience and are only one step removed from actual events, these visual representations may be able to capture and communicate the concrete experience in various ways.

"A good picture is equivalent to a good deed". As studies show success in thinking and learning visually instead of or in addition to traditional lectures and verbal description, a shift in technique is required. Students need to learn visually and teachers need to learn to teach visually. Using visual treatments in lessons enhances learning with varying degrees of success. How lessons with no graphics, still graphics, or animated graphics influence students with different prior knowledge levels as they attain procedural and descriptive knowledge. When prior knowledge is low, graphics, either still or animated, are better for learning descriptive facts than lessons with text only, yet learning procedural facts does not appear to differ with the use of text or graphics. However, students with a high level of prior knowledge of the subject responded better with the animated form of graphics in learning descriptive facts, but responded better with still graphics when learning procedural knowledge.

Students with different prior knowledge levels respond differently to contrasting presentation forms for achieving learning tasks, and that the effectiveness of visual design in learning is related to the prior knowledge of the students. Animated graphics are not superior to still graphics and may even be distracting to learning if the motions are inconsistent with how students process the visual information. Providing visual control of animated graphics enhances learning, particularly in males. Most learners prefer color visuals to black and white visuals, but that no significant difference in the amount of learning occurs except when color is related to the content to be learned. In addition, the study indicates that young learners prefer simple visuals and older students prefer complex visuals, yet simpler visuals are usually more effective regardless of the age group.

Additionally, students do not necessarily learn best from the kinds of pictures they prefer to view. Some of the researchers compared the use of a multimedia summary comprised of a sequence cof annotated illustrations depicting the steps in a process, with a 600-word text summary of the process. Also compared were the multimedia summary plus different amounts of text in knowledge retention and transfer. Results suggest that the multimedia summary is more effective than the verbal summary, and that the multimedia summary alone is more effective when it contains a small amount of text rather than a large amount of text. Their conclusions are that students can learn more effectively from a more concise summary, particularly when words and illustrations are presented together.

VARIATIONS IN VISUAL ELEMENTS

Many forms of graphics for instruction and enhancing understanding exist. Visual organisers that incorporate illustrations and text to depict patterns of concepts and ideas serve as organisational frameworks to promote thinking and learning. Frameworks assist learners in visualising how ideas may be related to prior knowledge, subordinate ideas, and information from other sources. Story maps that can be depicted as vertical or horizontal flow maps, Venn diagrams that prove useful in analysing similarities and differences between two or more concepts, and frameworks for webbing that encourage thought regarding the whole and its parts are examples of visual organisers.

Problem atiques use graphics as a language to identify complex and challenging problems by expanding the linear style traditionally used in teaching and learning to a non-linear format that expands the processing of information in a way that minimises cognitive overload. Other visual organisers include cause and effect frameworks, flow charts, and various types of charts such as checklists and scoring tools. The use of visuals in education, although consistently shown to aid in learning, must be carefully planned. The use of visuals that steer the learner to the exciting or entertaining aspects of presentation rather than encouraging thoughtful analysis of the underlying meaning may interfere with the intent of the lesson.

In addition, visuals must be properly used in the educational setting since visualisation alone does not function to maximise student achievement. The use of verbal and visual metaphors to complement visualised instruction is not always an effective instructional strategy.

13

PARENTS AND LEARNING

Everywhere there is pressure for children to learn more in school. The new economy demands that young people leave school with strong abilities to read, write, calculate and apply disciplined thought to the solution of problems. Citizenship in every society requires an understanding of the history, government and tradition of not only that society but of many others as well. More and more, the pursuit of individual happiness must begin with an educated view of a rapidly changing world.

As schools have been pressed to be more effective and more productive, out-of-school influences on academic learning have escalated in importance. Even where the school day and school year have been lengthened, the amount of time children spend in school during the first eighteen years of their lives is small compared to time spent with the family and the broader community. Fortunately, research on the family's influence on school learning has a substantial history, and we can settle upon basic premises with great confidence. With reasonable certainty we can state that poverty may statistically predict lower school performance, yet families that provide a stimulating, languagerich, supportive environment defy the odds of socio-economic circumstance.

Research on the relationships among families who constitute a school community leans heavily on a long body of sociological literature on communities of all types. Recently, however, primarily within the past decade, a strand of this sociological research has focused on schools as communities, and we are arriving at a set of understandings that may soon achieve the status of theory. As for what schools can do to affect family behaviours in ways that benefit children's learning, the research trail is shorter and less conclusive. There remains a great amount of experimentation, casting about to see what works.

Some initiatives have, in fact, worked, and we may report them, draw lessons from them, and generalise from them. While the home's influence on academic learning is significant, the quality and quantity of instruction and the child's own cognitive abilities are of equal or greater significance. There is a danger, then, in placing too much emphasis (or blame) on the family's contribution to the learning equation while forgiving weaknesses in the school. By the same token, ignoring the gains to be made by helping families improve the alterable curriculum of the home limits the potential effectiveness of the school.

Research on the curriculum of the home isolates specific patterns of family life that correspond with a child's success in academic learning. Specifically, studies have positively linked certain family practices with a child's learning.

PARENT CHILD RELATIONSHIP

Language development begins at birth and centres on the child's interactions with his or her parents. Several parent/child interactions are important in preparing the child to learn in school: talking to the infant, listening attentively to the child, reading to children and listening to them read, talking about what the parent and the child are reading, storytelling, daily conversation and letter writing. It is difficult to separate verbal interactions from the emotional and affective bonds that accompany them. For that reason, the parents' expressions of affection are included with verbal activities as essential to the parent/ child relationship. Also important is a constant demonstration by parents that learning is a natural part of life-joyful in its own right, part of the family experience, and especially exhilarating when encountered through discovery at such places as museums, zoos and historical sites.

Do not all families talk about everyday events? Perhaps, but there is great variation in the quality and quantity of that interaction. Is the underlying tone of the conversation positive, supportive? Does the conversation flow in both directions-between parent and child? Do both parties listen as well as speak? As children grow older, the time spent in conversation with parents may decline. Daily touchstone routines, such as a relaxed dinnertime, provide continued opportunity for family conversation.

A consistent emotional bond between parent and child, seen in expressions of affection, renders the child more psychologically equipped to meet the stresses and challenges of life outside the home, especially in school. Affection is also a social lubricant for the family, cementing relationships and helping children develop positive attitudes about school and learning. When families talk about books, newspapers, magazines and television programmes, children's minds are treated to the delight of verbal inquiry. The drama of unfolding events and the clash of differing opinions open doors to intellectual pursuit for children.

Curiosity is kept alive. Stimulating the child's desire to discover, to think through new situations and to vigorously exchange opinions, is fostered also by family visits to libraries, museums, zoos, historical sites and cultural events. Vocabulary is the building block of thought and expression. All small children love to try new words. In some families, exploration with words is encouraged; in fact, it is an ongoing source of family pleasure. But some children are exposed to ridicule when they mispronounce or misuse a new word; their love for words may be extinguished, and they may feel constrained to cling to a limited vocabulary.

Parents can be taught, through role-playing techniques, to be good listeners with their children, to extend meagre daily dialogue into rich family conversation, and to play word games that promote an interest in vocabulary. They can also be encouraged to visit museums and other stimulating places and to engage their children in the excitement of discovery. Parents can even learn the importance of affectionate contact with their children, especially at times when the child may be fearful or anxious-when leaving the home in the morning and when going to sleep at night, for example.

Busy families can fall out of the habit of daily conversation. Asking parents to spend at least one minute each day in private conversation with each child, primarily listening to the child tell about his or her day without distraction from other family members or television, will demonstrate how rare and precious such moments can be. Sharing these experiences with other parents, in small-group settings, amplifies their impact.

ROUTINE OF FAMILY LIFE

Studies find that the routine of family life, the daily

interactions between parents and children, the types of hobbies and recreational activities the family enjoys, all have a bearing on children's readiness for school learning. When children from lowincome families do things with their parents on weekends, have dinner as a family and engage in family hobbies, they make up for some of the disadvantages of poverty, and their school performance improves. How time is used is an important consideration in the homes of high-achieving students.

While the parents encourage their children's independence, they do so with a constant eye on how successfully their children are managing their freedom. They praise productivity and accomplishment. They challenge their children to use time wisely. Children in these homes are accustomed to calendars, schedules, grocery lists, to do' lists, household chores, reading, studying and playing mentally challenging games. One study found that highachieving students spend about twenty hours each week outside of school in constructive learning activities, often with the support, guidance or participation of their parents. These activities might include homework, music practice, reading, writing, visiting museums and engaging in learning activities sponsored by youth organisations.

When the family sets aside time each day for children to study, rather than asking children to study only when required to do so by their teachers, the children learn that studying is valued by the family. Studying and learning become a natural part of family life. Children do their best when they operate within the boundaries of the family's settled routine. Some activities are daily touchstones; they define the flow of time and enable children to attend to activities of high priority, such as studying, reading and talking with family members.

Eating meals at about the same time each day, going to bed at about the same time, and studying and reading at about the same time will establish a productive and healthful rhythm for children's lives. Children also need a predictably quiet and well-lit place to study and read. They benefit from family interest in hobbies, games and other activities that exercise the mind and engage the child in interaction with other people. A daily routine that includes a time to study and read, a home environment that provides a quiet place to study, and family activities that include games and hobbies which engage children's minds and provide interaction with other family members characterise a home where children are prepared by habit and value to learn in school.

FAMILY EXPECTATIONS

Studies find that children do better in school when their parents set high but realistic academic standards for them. Parents of good learners also place importance on verbal interaction; they question their children to prompt further thought and expression, they challenge them to use new words, and they expect them to speak with precision. Families with high expectations for their children's school performance also provide consistent guidance and support for schooling.

They are aware of their children's progress and interested in the academic route their children are plotting. Researchers find that a strong work ethic contributes to success in school. Also important is a family attitude that accomplishments result from effort rather than innate ability or 'playing the system'. Further, children benefit when their parents are attentive to their whereabouts, know their friends, monitor their televiewing, and maintain contact with their teachers.

Several exercises can be employed to help parents understand the standards and examples they are setting for their children. One exercise is to simply sketch a typical weekly schedule of the child's activities beyond the school day. When does the child usually study? Read? Play with friends? Watch television? Examining the schedule gives a clue to the relative priority the family is giving to each activity. Parents often look to teachers for guidelines.

The expectation that children spend a minimum amount of time studying and reading each day (perhaps ten minutes for each grade level) is such a guideline. The dangers of television may be exaggerated, but when children watch television more than ninety minutes a day, school performance falls off. At some point the amount of time given to television is being robbed from a more productive activity, such as reading or studying. Parents sometimes need to be reminded that children benefit from varied activities, including recreational and social activities, and that schoolwork need not replace these activities. Studying and reading, however, should come first.

Parents can help their children develop their own schedule each week, allowing them to set aside time for fun if they have first allotted adequate time for study. Perhaps the most difficult challenge for a parent is to know when a child is doing his or her best. Setting high but realistic expectations is easier said than done. When it comes to schoolwork, however, a good approach is to consider the child's study habits and attitude toward school rather than focusing solely on the child's marks. This is not to say that marks are unimportant; but marks can be deceptive. Some children achieve reasonably high marks with little effort, and fail to develop good study habits as a consequence.

Other children work hard but never achieve the highest marks; they may be doing their best and their dedication to their learning deserves praise. Comparing siblings is a particular pitfall for parents. A simple rule for parents is that they always know where their children are, what they are doing, and who they are with. Being sure to meet their child's friends and knowing the names and addresses of the friends' parents is a good prerequisite for allowing a child to spend time with a peer. Regular communication with their children's teachers is equally important.

COMMUNICATION AT SCHOOL AND HOME

Students do best when parents and teachers understand each other's expectations and stay in touch with one another regarding the child's learning habits, attitudes toward school, social interactions and academic progress. The school, through the leadership of its administration and the school's policies and programmes, can create an atmosphere conducive to communication and provide convenient opportunities for communication. Teachers are most inclined to initiate communication with parents when they perceive that administrators value such communication, their colleagues are supportive of parental involvement, and the parents seem appreciative of the outreach.

Communication between the school and the home is most effective when it flows in both directions, and schools should distinguish between efforts to inform parents and opportunities to communicate with parents. The following examples of school/home communication provide convenient and effective communication between parents and school personnel.

Benefits of Communication

Report cards: Report cards are typically used by teachers to inform parents about the child's progress in school. But report cards can become two-way by including the parents' report of the child's progress at home with such school-related topics as: willingness to do homework; reading for pleasure; moderation of televiewing; and attitude toward learning. The cards might also encourage parents to note specific concerns or request conferences.

Schools newsletter: Many schools publish newsletters. To encourage two-way communication, ask parents to write articles for the newsletter. What tips can parents give for helping kids with homework? What family activities would parents like to share? Has the family visited a museum, historical site or other place of educational value?

Happy-Grams: Print pads of Happy-Grams for teachers to send notes to parents complimenting students for specific achievements and behaviours. Because teachers also appreciate notes of kindness, distribute pads of Happy-Grams to parents. Print blank Happy-Grams forms in the newsletter. Parents can clip the forms from the newsletter and send notes to teachers.

Parent/teacher conference: Designate a certain time when teachers are available for walkin conferences. Some schools set aside thirty minutes before school each morning (or on certain days of the week) when all teachers are available to parents.

Bulletin board: Place a bulletin board, especially for parents, at the main entry to the school. Parents can conveniently check the board for notes about parent meetings, suggestions for helping children with homework, notices about family activities and calendars of important events.

Home links from the classroom: Parents like to know what their child is learning at school. A weekly take-home that lists a few topics covered at school that week is helpful. The take-home may also include examples of parent/child activities that would be related to what is being learned at school.

Assignment notebooks: A notebook in which students record each day's assignments (and perhaps also keep track of the marks they earn) is helpful in keeping students on track. When parents are asked to view, date and initial the notebook and the teacher routinely examines the notebook, a good student/teacher/parent communication link is established.

'Parental involvement' is an all-encompassing and imprecise term that includes everything from the parent's child-rearing practices at home to the parent's participation in events held at school. Included in the child-rearing practices may be those aspects of parenting that have particular application to the child's performance in school (the curriculum of the home), as well as more general practices of feeding, nurturing and caring for children. Included in the category of events held at the school would be everything from attendance at athletic competitions to participation in parent/teacher conferences and completion of extensive parent education courses. A commonly accepted typology of parental involvement includes the following categories:

- — Parenting (caring for and nurturing the child);
- — Communicating (maintaining a flow of information between parent and school);
- — Volunteering (helping at the school);
- — Learning at home (supporting and supplementing the instruction of the school);
- — Decision-making (part of the school's decision-making structure); and
- — Collaboration with the community at large (representing the school in partnerships with other organisations).

Researchers point to impediments to parental involvement: Defining too narrowly the scope of parental involvement to include only attendance at formal meetings and other activities held at the school, assigning too little importance to the parent's relationship with the child at home. Low expectation on the part of school personnel, for example assuming that single parents or low-income parents are not able to provide the support and guidance their children require.

Lack of preparation for teachers to enable them to involve parents in ways that facilitate school learning. Occupational obstacles that make it difficult for parents to be available at times convenient to school personnel. Parental attitudes about or experiences with schools that make them resistant to contact with school personnel. Because a school may expect only limited access to and influence over most parents, it should carefully select the ways it expects parents to be involved.

In general, parents' involvement in curriculum-of-the-home activities with their children is more beneficial to the children's school learning than involvement with activities at the school. A parent's relationship with other parents in the child's school, and the parent's communication with the child's classroom teacher are, however, important to the child's success in school. And the quality of the school may depend upon the willingness of some parents to be at the table when institutional decisions are made. The typology shown here can provide the school a good framework for developing a range of parent-involvement programmes and activities.

EDUCATION OF PARENTS

Parent education includes home visits by parent educators, group sessions led by previously trained parents, and workshops and courses taught by experts. The home-visit model is typically directed at parents of pre-school children and includes explanations of the child's developmental stage and examples of appropriate parent-child activities. Parent group sessions enable parents to learn in a small-group setting, carry out activities with their children between sessions, and discuss their experience with other parents. When led by other parents rather than teachers or experts, these parent groups are collegial and non-threatening.

Workshops and courses conducted by experts-educators, psychologists or paediatricians, for example-have the advantage of research-based content and access to professional knowledge. Research shows that programmes that teach mothers to improve the quality of cognitive stimulation and verbal interaction produce immediate effects on the child's intellectual development. When parents learn systems for monitoring and guiding their children's outof-school time, the children do better in school.

Schools that teach parents ways to reinforce school learning at home find that students are more motivated to learn and attend school more regularly. Parent education programmes enhance teacher/parent communication and the attitude of parents toward the school. Efforts to encourage family reading activities result in the children's improved reading skills and interest in reading. Programmes that include both parents and children are more effective than programmes that deal with only the parents. Home-visit programmes are most effective when combined with group meetings with other parents.

The obstacles to school-sponsored parent education can be daunting. Some parents are not receptive to the good intentions of parent education providers, and recruiting participants for parent education programmes can be a frustrating process. Teachers usually have quite enough to do caring for their students; working with parents can be seen as an added burden. So the twin problems of parent education are: (a) providing personnel to organise and deliver the parent education programmes; and (b) attracting parents to the programmes.

Home-visit models are labour-intensive and therefore expensive. But because they are directed at the parents of preschool children, they have the advantage of a parent clientele that is very receptive to parent education. Taking the programme to the parents at their home makes home visits convenient for parents, places the educator in the natural setting of the home, and enables the parent educator to focus on one family at a time. Small-group sessions led by previously trained parents are inexpensive, encourage parental attachment to the school and allow parents to share experiences and assist one another. On the other hand, attracting parents to sessions offered outside the home requires substantial attention to recruitment.

Strategies for Schools and Teachers

- — Partner with other organisations that can affect parenting in the pre-school years through home visits and other efforts: paediatricians, public health, community organisations and churches, for example.
- — Make a specific list of what the school wants from parents according to the age group of the child, then organise parent education around this list.
- — Publish, inform, monitor, support and assist with homework policies.
- — Use parents to organise, recruit and lead other parents.
- — Consider field-tested, proven models and curricula.
- — Focus on the curriculum of the home.

FAMILY/SCHOOL RELATIONSHIPS

Family/school relationships may be viewed as corresponding to three historical phases of economic development. In the first phase, typical of agricultural societies, but also of some families in all societies, the family lives at a subsistence level, relying on children for work (or, more commonly in modern States, for emotional comfort). In this situation, the family may limit the educational potential of the child, and the school's role is to expand the possibilities for the child's development.

In the second phase, common to the industrial economy, the goals of the family and the school converge, with both institutions seeking the improvement of the child's ultimate economic situation. In the third phase, that of post-industrial affluence, parents find the demands of child-rearing competing with the pursuits of their adult lives. They expect the school to fill the void. In modern societies, we find all three types of families described below. Placing any family in a category can be an injustice to that family, but characterising common family situations and strategies for engaging them can be instructive.

Some families, usually those living in poverty, are severely pressed by the demands of everyday life. They often possess limited parenting skills, lack social contacts and have access to few models of good child-rearing practices. They may be intimidated by teachers and see the school as a bearer of bad news. They are likely to perceive that they are targets of discrimination. Parent education programmes that show them how to relate to their children are helpful, but first they need genuine, personal expressions of goodwill from school personnel and other parents. They must be engaged within a nonthreatening, positive and supportive social context, often provided by other parents rather than by school personnel.

The child-centred family understands the necessity of schooling to the economic betterment of their children. These families often fear that the school is inadequately attentive to their children. They are frustrated by what they perceive as negative social influences, and they may cast aspersions upon other parents, whom they see as lax and uncaring. On the other hand, these parents are willing to work for their children's school, provide leadership among parents, and serve as surrogate parents for neglected children. They are best engaged by giving them constructive roles in the school and opportunities to work with other parents.

The challenge for the school is to channel the efforts of child-centred parents toward activities that benefit the academic and personal development of their own children and of other children. Child-centred parents make wonderful leaders for parent education programmes.

Busy professional parents value schooling but are sometimes so absorbed by their careers and personal interests that they are disengaged from close involvement in their children's lives. To compensate, they place their children in the best schools, thus entrusting their children to what they see as competent, hired professionals. They do the same in other aspects of their children's lives, providing experiences for their children through programmes and services they employ. These talented, well-connected parents possess financial resources, education, social contacts and professional skills. They must be re-engaged with their children by means that are nearly spiritual.

Their conversion comes through the heart. If directed into intimate relationships with their children, they are reminded of the satisfaction that they deny themselves by relegating childrearing responsibilities to others.

FAMILIES AND COMMUNITIES

In many societies, bonds of community no longer envelop the families of children who happen to attend the same school. This means that parents do not necessarily associate with one another away from the school, and their contact with one another in connection with the school is very limited. As a consequence, children spend their school days sitting next to, influencing and being influenced by other children, yet the parents of these children do not know one another. Many children spend a great portion of their out-of-school hours alone or with other children, not under the supervision of caring adults.

Children benefit when the adults around them share basic values about child-rearing, communicate with one another, and give the children consistent support and guidance. Social capital, the asset available to children that resides in the relationships among adults in their lives, depends upon face-to-face association of these adults. A school that views itself as a community of its constituents (school personnel, students, families of students), rather than an organisation, is more likely to encourage the social interactions that lead to the accumulation of social capital.

A school is capable of forming and nurturing community among its constituents-school personnel and the families of When the families of children in a school its students. A framework for building a school community will include ways to articulate commonly held values about education, draw parents together with other parents and with teachers, and enable the school to function as an institutional champion of the families' educational desires for their children.

Elements of a programme to enhance community in a school would include:

- *Representation*: Parents are included in decision-making groups at the school.
- *Educational values*: Parents and teachers together articulate the educational values common to the school, and the school's goals and its expectations of students, teachers and parents flow from these shared values.
- *Communication*: Two-way communication between the home and the school is afforded through a variety of means, including parent/teacher/student conferences, telephone conversations, notes and assignment notebooks.
- *Education*: Education programmes for teachers and parents are provided in order to constantly improve everyone's ability to help children succeed.
- *Common experience*: All students, and often their parents and teachers, are engaged in collective events or connected to common strains in the educational programme that unite them and allow them to share common educational experiences.
- *Association*: The school arranges opportunities for groups of school-community members to associate with one another, particularly for reasons relative to the purposes of the school. For example, groups of parents with other parents, groups of parents and teachers, younger students with older students, and intergenerational mentoring between students and adult volunteers (including 'grandparents').

When a school decides to reach out to the community to tap resources, it is wise to first determine its students' unmet needs, then approach community organisations to negotiate the delivery of services that might meet these needs. Student needs not easily met by the school's own resources might include: basic family needs (clothing, food, housing, child care); health needs (vaccination, examination, dental care); behavioural therapy; recreation; tutoring; psychological testing; mentoring; equipment for disabilities; respite care; opportunities relative to special talents or interests (scientific, musical, artistic, athletic, literary). Once student needs have been listed and matched with a catalogue of community resources, students and their families can be systematically connected with appropriate services.

14

CREATIVE TEACHING

Teacher proofing have gained adherents in the 1990s' as increasing numbers of schools continue to implement scripted curricula that turn teachers into script readers. Scripted teacher-proof curricula do not rely either on teachers' creative potential or their subject matter expertise; the message of these programmes seems to be 'if you can perform well from a script' you can teach.

Yet critics of such programmes note that the best teachers apply immense creativity and profound content knowledge to their jobs' both in advance preparation and from moment to moment while in the classroom. Although scripted approaches have documented improvements in test scores' critics argue that scripted instruction emphasises lowerorder skills that are particularly easy to measure with standardised tests. Advocates of creative teaching argue that it results in deeper understanding among learners' a form of learning that is more difficult to quantitatively assess.

Thus under-performing schools are faced with two very different visions for reform. Scripted approaches attempt to teacher proof the curriculum by rigidly specifying teacher actions' and essentially removing all creativity and professional judgment from the classroom. Creative teaching suggests a very different vision:

teachers are knowledgeable and expert professionals' and are granted creative autonomy in their classrooms. Our economy is increasingly based on knowledge workers and a "creative class"' and these economic trends seem to require creative teaching that emphasises learning for deeper understanding' rather than mastery of lower-order facts and skills.

Scripted teaching is consistent with a long tradition of comparing teaching to performance. Scripted instruction is clearly performative: teachers stand "on stage" in front of the classroom "audience"; the lectures and student exchanges are "scripts" for the performance; teachers should "rehearse" their presentations; and the teacher/ performer must work hard to hold the attention of the audience' with timing' stage presence' and enthusiasm. The teaching as performance metaphor encourages teachers to think of themselves as actors on a stage' enacting a performance for their students.

This metaphor emphasises important skills for teachers' such as presentation' delivery' voice' movement' and timing. Yet the metaphor of teaching as performance is problematic' because it suggests a solo performer reading from a script' with the students as the passive' observing audience. These uses of the performance metaphor reduce teaching to an individualistic focus on the teacher as an actor. Like scripted instruction' the performance metaphor suggests that an effective actor could be an excellent teacher even without understanding anything.

Creative teaching is better conceived of as improvisational performance. Conceiving of teaching as im-provisation emphasises the interactional and responsive creativity of a teacher working together with a unique group of students. In particular' effective classroom discussion is improvisational' because the flow of the class is unpredictable and emerges from the actions of all participants' both teachers and students.

Creative teaching is disciplined improvisation because it always occurs within broad structures and frameworks. Expert teachers use routines and activity structures more than novice teachers; but they are able to invoke and apply these routines in a creative' improvisational fashion. The most effective classroom interaction balances structure and script with flexibility and improvisation. Educators who hold to constructivist principles are those most likely to be critical of scripted instruction; and advocates of scripted instruction are often critical of constructivist theory and practice.

TEACHING AS IMPROVISATION

In improvisational theater' a group of actors creates a performance without using a script. Some groups specialise in short skits only a few minutes long' and others specialise in fully improvised one- or two-act plays of an hour or more. These performances emerge from unpredictable and unscripted dialogue' on stage and in front of an audience.

The basic insight of constructivism is that learning is a creative improvisational process. Recent work that extends constructivist theory to classroom collaboration conceives of learning as co-construction. Socio-culturalists focus on how knowledge is learned in and by groups. Socio-cultural studies have demonstrated the importance of social interaction in groups' and have shown that a microgenetic focus on improvised interactional process can reveal many insights into how learning takes place. A central theme in the socio-cultural tradition is the focus on the group rather than the individual. Socio-culturalists analyse the entire group as their unit of analysis; cognition is "an aspect of human socio-cultural activity" rather than "a property of individuals".

Socio-culturalists hold that groups can be said to "learn" as collectives' and that knowledge can be a possession or property of a group' not only of the individual participants in the group. For example' actions taken by the crew of a ship to make their way into a harbor' but with a broken navigational system that forced the crew to collectively improvise. A transcript of their interactions indicated that no one crew member understood the complete system that they had improvised or exactly why it was succeeding; thus' the crew's solution to the problem they collectively faced emerged from ensemble improvisation' and this emergent solution can be thought of as a form of collective learning.

In socio-cultural and social constructivist theory' effective teaching must be improvisational' because if the classroom is scripted and directed by the teacher' the students cannot co-construct their own knowledge. Such talk is open ended' is not structured in advance' and is an interaction among peers' where any participant can contribute equally to the flow of the interaction. Classrooms are not as improvisational when the teacher controls the flow of the class' strictly limiting when students can talk and how much impact what they say can have on the flow of the class.

Latter type of classroom discourse with the traditional classroom' to contrast it with the more improvisational' collaborative classrooms associated with constructivist and inquiry-based methods. The sociocultural perspective implies that the entire classroom is improvising together; and it holds that the most effective learning results when the classroom proceeds in an open' improvisational fashion' as children are allowed to experiment' interact' and participate in the collaborative construction of their own knowledge. In improvisational teaching' learning is a shared social activity' and is collectively managed by all participants' not only the teacher.

In improvising' the teacher creates a dialogue with the students' giving them freedom to creatively construct their own knowledge' while providing the elements of structure that effectively scaffold that co-constructive process. The students propose different answers throughout the discussion; the teacher does not evaluate any given answer' but instead facilitates a collaborative improvisation among the students' with the goal of guiding them toward the social construction of their own knowledge. In fact' she has guided them to learning that was not in her original problem' which was simply to ask them to come with the "divide by two" rule.

In addition' the students have begun to learn about variables' and have learned a fundamental insight about fractions that will help them when they begin to multiply by fractions. Although an experienced teacher may have encountered most of the potential student answers in prior years' a teacher cannot know exactly which answer will be proposed on any given day. And even with years of experience' a teacher cannot predict how the rest of the class will respond to a proposed answer; the flow of the discussion is collaboratively determined by all of the students responding to each other' and the knowledge that is co-constructed by the students emerges from the improvisational flow of dialogue.

The classroom is collaboratively creative; the teacher is not the sole creative force' but rather a facilitator for the entire group's creativity. To create an improvisational classroom' the teacher must have a high degree of pedagogical content knowledge-to respond creatively to unexpected student queries' a teacher must have a more profound understanding of the material than if the teacher is simply reciting a pre-planned lecture or script.

An unexpected student query often requires the teacher to think quickly and creatively' accessing material that may not have been studied the night before in preparation for this class; and it requires the teacher to quickly and improvisationally be able to translate his or her own knowledge of the subject into a form that will communicate with that student's level of knowledge.

In addition to pedagogical content knowledge' it is less widely recognised that classroom collaboration requires the teacher to skillfully manage group improvisation. Improvisational skill is required to manage the participatory aspects of social interaction - turn taking' the timing and sequence of turns' participant roles and relationships' the degree of simultaneity of participation' and rights of participants to speak. It is also required at the pedagogical content level-to notice and comment on connections among students and with the material. A better understanding of improvisational performance can help us understand the creative processes involved in collaborative learning.

In addition to lectures' IRE recitations' and solitary work on problems' many teachers use the technique of collaborating groups' where a group of two to four students is placed in a circle and given an assignment to solve collectively. In many cases' the members of the group are graded on the performance of the entire group as well as on their own performance' providing them with an incentive to contribute to the group's overall learning. Social constructivists believe that these groups are effective because they provide an opportunity for the improvisational collaboration that results in deeper understanding.

When children's groups were child directed-without an adult present-the children often spontaneously improvised' developing their plans on the fly by trying out new ideas for actions or dialogue. Once an interesting idea emerged from the improvisation' the children recognised it and then moved to a more global' metacommunicative level to figure out how to integrate the newly emergent idea into their evolving collaborative creation. However' when adults participated in a play-crafting session' they never joined in this improvisational planning and elaboration. Rather' they typically presented their ready-made play plans and scripts to the children' who then simply executed the adult's script.

Children instinctively improvise together' but that it is difficult for adults to learn how to manage a collaborative improvisation in class. It seems inefficient to many critics-a waste of time' and an abdication of teacher responsibility. Like many neo-Piagetian social constructivists' Cobb argued that this interaction is multivocal: containing multiple perspectives rather than the single "right" perspective of the teacher. These two students are both getting to the correct answer' but are using different methods.

Even though the children do not appear to be listening to each other' they reciprocally influence each others' arguments' and both of them make conceptual advances by elaborating their assumptions. By exchanging views and working toward identifying what is shared by their two solutions' they gradually construct a robust and profound understanding of subtracting numbers' which is more profound than if they had been taught the rote method of "borrowing" with scripted instruction and then been made to drill-and-practice using worksheets at their desks.

Connects the Piagetian sociocognitive insight that children learn from the conflict and controversy of peer interaction with a Bakhtinian focus on multiple voices' or heteroglossia. Improvising ensembles are similarly heteroglossic' as the voices of the performers meld together through a give and take whereby intersubjectivity is collaboratively emergent. Children learn from collaborative discourse because there are multiple perspectives' and this form of learning can only work if the group is improvisational' with no predetermined outcome and no preset script.

Collaborative learning only works if there is a give-and-take' the mutual responsiveness associated with jazz and improv theater groups. Student discussion must be allowed to take its own course' so that group learning can emerge from the interaction of the group.

Structure of Disciplined Improvisation

Even when teachers are following a rather rigid script' there is always some residual requirement to improvise responses to students in the class. Even when teachers followed conventionalised classroom routines they subconsciously and effortlessly improvised variations on the routine in response to the unique demands of each classroom. When a student's response is unexpected' the teacher has to improvise a way to respond to the question and then return to his or her own script for the class. Thus' even relatively scripted in-struction could benefit from a better understanding of improvisational performance.

Disciplined improvisation acknowledges the need for a curriculum -there must be some structure to the classroom performance. Disciplined improvisation is "a dynamic process involving a combination of planning and improvisation". Improvisational classroom discourse revealed that collaborative dialogues are midway between ritual and the extreme improvisationality of everyday small talk. In Erickson's phrase' lessons are "structured conversations'" in which dialogue is largely improvisational' but within overall task and participation structures. Interactive teaching is best conceived of as compositionimprovisation combined.

In disciplined improvisation' teachers locally improvise within an overall global structure. Professional staged improvisation always occurs within a structure. Jazz ensembles improvise using the framework of a familiar song; improv theater groups use broad outlines to help provide their 30-minute improvisations with an overall plot structure. In addition to these broad overall structures' improvisation works because all participants have internalised many shared conventions.

The influential medieval performances of the commedia dell'arte were improvisations within an overall plot structure known as a scenario. The dialogue was not scripted in advance; no scripts have ever been found by historians. However' many scenarios were written down and have been preserved; these specify the sequence of scenes' which characters are to appear in each scene' what happens in that scene and how it relates to the overall flow of the plot. In modern theater' overall structures are quite common in long-form improvisation' when ensembles perform a fully improvised 30- to 60-minute play.

Although dialogue and characters are not determined in advance' the actors often choose an overall framework for the plot structure. For example' in the mid-1990s Chicago group Sitcom' all actors were trained in the typical elements of sitcom structures-three acts separated by commercials' and common plot structures like "false crisis" or "mis-understood overhearing" that are resolved in the third act. When teachers organise collaborating groups of students' they face a tension familiar to improvising ensembles: between the need for pre-existing structures and the need to leave flexibility for collaborative emergence to occur.

The most effective collaborating groups are those that are partially structured' in careful ways' by the teacher. The most effective collaborations involve some structure' but not too much' and are of a type appropriate to the learning task. For example' the teacher may constrain the collaboration by instructing students in specific conversational strategies or requiring them to follow a certain sequence of actions; or the teacher may assign specific functional roles' such as "facilitator'" to individual students. If' on the one hand' teachers do nothing to structure a collaborating group of students' the students can easily become anxious as they become overwhelmed by the challenges of the task.

If' on the other hand' the collaboration is overly structured' the students are prevented from co-constructing their own knowledge' thus' preventing the benefits that collaboration was intended to accomplish. Disciplined improvisation seems best suited for unstructured tasks with no clear-cut procedures or answers' when effective interaction depends on "a mutual exchange process in which ideas' hypotheses' strategies' and speculations are shared".

Teachers have to manage the balance between structure and improvisation differently than a theater group. Teachers cannot afford to fail too much of the time because students' learning is at stake; they will probably always need to have more structure than improv performances. Educational theorists have proposed a variety of terms for the structures used in disciplined improvisation: scaffolds' activity formats' pedagogical frameworks' interactional routines. Examinations of improv theater games and formats can help us better understand the relationship between curriculum structures' classroom processes' and learning.

The most effective teachers are those that can effectively use a wide range of degrees of structure' shifting between scripts' scaffolds' and activity formats as the material and the students seem to require. These shifts in themselves are improvisational responses to the unique needs of that class. When teachers participate in curriculum development' they participate in the creation of these guiding structures. Because of the teacher's active participation' the structures that result are more likely to lend themselves to disciplined improvisation. Rather than performers of curricula'· teachers become creative designers of curricula.

Teaching has always involved the creative appropriation of curricula within the situated practice of a given classroom. The curriculum is a cultural tool' and like all such tools' it carries constraints and affordances that always allow creative improvisation in their application. Yet we need to better understand the relation between curriculum and classroom practice. Studying how improvisation takes place within the structures of performance can help us better theorise the relation between curriculum and classroom practice.

15

EFFECTIVE EDUCATIONAL PRACTICES

The home environment has a powerful effect on what children and youth learn within and outside school. This environment is considerably more powerful than the parents' income and education in influencing what children learn in the first six years of life and during the twelve years of primary and secondary education. One major reason that parental influence is so strong is that, from infancy until the age of 18, children spend approximately 92% of their time outside school under the influence of their parents. Co-operative efforts by parents and educators to modify these alterable academic conditions in the home have strong, beneficial effects on learning. In twenty-nine controlled studies, 91% of the comparisons favoured children in such programmes over non-participant control groups.

Sometimes called 'the curriculum of the home', the home environment refers to informed parent/child conversations about school and everyday events; encouragement and discussion of leisure reading; monitoring and critical review of television viewing and peer activities; deferral of immediate gratification to accomplish long-term goals; expressions of affection and interest in the child's academic and other progress as a person; and perhaps, among such unremitting efforts, laughter and caprice.

Reading to children and discussing everyday events prepare them for academic activities before attending school. Co-operation between educators and parents can support these approaches. Educators can suggest specific activities likely to promote children's learning at home and in school. They can also develop and organise large-scale teacher/parent programmes to promote academically stimulating conditions and activities outside the school in a systematic manner.

DIRECT TEACHING

Many studies show that direct teaching can be effective in promoting student learning. The process emphasises systematic sequencing of lessons, a presentation of new content and skills, guided student practice, the use of feedback and independent practice by students. The traits of teachers employing effective direct instruction include clarity, task orientation, enthusiasm and flexibility.

Effective direct teachers also clearly organise their presentations and occasionally use student ideas. The use of direct teaching can be traced to the turn of the last century; it is what many citizens and parents expect to see in classrooms.

Done well, it can yield consistent and substantial results. Whole-class teaching of diverse groups may mean that lessons are too advanced for slower students and too repetitive for the quick. In the last decade or two, moreover, theorists have tried to transfer more control of lesson planning and completion to students themselves so that they 'learn to learn', as several subsequent practices exemplify. Six phased functions of direct teaching work well:

a) Daily review, homework check and, if necessary, reteaching;

b) Presentation of new content and skills in small steps;

c) Guided student practice with close teacher monitoring;

d) Corrective feedback and instructional reinforcement;

e) Independent practice in work at the desk and in homework with a high (more than 90%) success rate; and

f) Weekly and monthly reviews.

g) Advance organisers

More than a dozen studies have shown that, when teachers explain how new ideas in the current lesson relate to ideas in previous lessons and other prior learning, students can connect the old with the new, which helps them to better remember and understand. Similarly, alerting them to the learning of key-points allows them to concentrate on the most crucial parts of the lessons. Advance organisers help students focus on key ideas by enabling them to anticipate which points are important to learn. Understanding the sequence or continuity of subject-matter development, moreover, can be motivating. If students simply learn one isolated idea after another, the subject-matter may appear arbitrary.

Given a 'mental road map' of what they have accomplished, where they are presently, and where they are going can avoid unpleasant surprises and help them to set realistic goals. Similar effects can be accomplished by goal-setting, overviewing and pre-testing before lessons that sensitise students to important points and questions that they will encounter in textbooks and will be presented by teachers.

It may also be useful to show how what is being learned solves problems that exist in the world outside school and that students are likely to meet in life. For example, human biology that features nutrition and its implications for food choices is likely to be more interesting than abstract biology. Teachers and textbooks can sometimes make effective use of graphic advance organisers. Maps, timetables, flow charts depicting the sequence of activities, and other such devices may be worth hundreds of words. They may also be easier to remember.

TEACHING OF LEARNING STRATEGIES

In the 1980s, cognitive research on teaching sought ways to encourage self-monitoring, self-teaching or 'meta-cognition' to foster achievement and independence. Skills are important, but the learner's monitoring and management of his or her own learning have primacy. This approach transfers part of the direct teaching functions of planning, allocating time and review to learners. Being aware of what goes on in one's mind during learning is a critical first step to effective independent learning. Some students have been found to lack this self-awareness and must be taught the skills necessary to monitor and regulate their own learning. Many studies have demonstrated that positive effects can accrue from developed skills.

Students with a repertoire of learning strategies can measure their own progress towards explicit goals. When students use these strategies to strengthen their opportunities for learning, they simultaneously increase their skills of self-awareness, personal control and positive self-evaluation. Three possible phases of teaching about learning strategies include:

a) Modelling, in which the teacher exhibits the desired behaviour;

b) Guided practice, in which students perform with help from the teacher; and

c) Application, during which students act independently of the teacher.

As an example, a successful programme of 'reciprocal teaching' fosters reading comprehension by having students take turns in leading dialogues on pertinent features of texts. By as-suming the roles of planning and monitoring ordinarily exercised by teachers, students learn self-management. Perhaps that is why tutors learn from tutoring, and why it is said: 'To learn something well, teach it.'

TUTORING

Tutoring gears learning to student needs. It has yielded large learning effects in several dozen studies. It yields particularly large effects in mathematics-perhaps because of the subject's well-defined sequence and organisation. If students fall behind in a fast-paced mathematics class, they may never catch up unless their particular problems are identified and remedied. This individualised assessment and follow-up process is the virtue of tutoring and other means of adaptive instruction.

Peer tutoring (tutoring of slower or younger students by more advanced students) appears to work nearly as well as teacher tutoring; with sustained student practice it might be equal to teacher tutoring in some cases. Significantly, peer tutoring promotes effective learning in tutors as well as tutees. The need to organise one's thoughts in order to impart them intelligibly to others, the need to become conscious of the value of time, and the need to learn managerial and social skills are probably the main reasons for benefits to the tutor.

Even slower-learning students and those with disabilities can be in the position of teaching to others if they are given the extra time and practice that may be required to master a skill. This can give them a positive experience and increase their feelings of self-esteem.

MASTERY LEARNING

More than fifty studies show that careful sequencing, monitoring and control of the learning process raise the learning rate. Pre-testing helps determine what should be studied; this allows the teacher to avoid assigning material that has already been mastered or for which the student does not yet have the prerequisite skills. Ensuring that students achieve mastery of initial steps in the sequence helps ensure that they will make satisfactory progress in subsequent, more advanced steps. Frequent assessment of progress informs teachers and students when additional time and corrective remedies are needed.

Mastery learning appears to work best when the subject-matter is well organised. Because of its emphasis on outcomes and careful monitoring of progress, mastery learning can save learners' time. It allows more time and remediation for students who need it. It also enables faster learners to skip material they already know. Since mastery learning suits instruction to the needs of each student, it can work better than giving the whole class the same lesson at the same time.

Such whole-class teaching may be too hard for some learners and too easy for others. Mastery learning programmes require special planning, materials and procedures. Teachers must be prepared to identify the components of instruction, develop assessment strategies so that individual students are appropriately placed in the instructional continuum, and provide re-inforcement and corrective feedback-while continuously engaging students in lessons.

CO-OPERATIVE LEARNING

As shown by more than fifty studies, learning proceeds more effectively than usual when exchanges among teachers and learners are frequent and specifically directed towards students' problems and interests. In whole-class instruction, only one person can speak at a time, and shy or slow-learning students may be reluctant to speak at all. When students work in groups of two to four, however, each group member can participate extensively, individual problems are more likely to become clear and to be remedied (sometimes with the teacher's assistance), and learning can accelerate.

With justification, co-operative learning has become widespread. Not only can it increase academic achievement, but also it has other virtues. By working in small groups, students learn teamwork, how to give and receive criticism, and how to plan, monitor and evaluate their individual and joint activities with others.

It appears that modern workplaces increasingly require such partial delegation of authority, group management and co-operative skills. Like modern managers, teachers may need to become more like facilitators, consultants and evaluators, rather than supervisors. Nonetheless, researchers do not recommend that co-operative learning take up the whole school day; the use of a variety of procedures, rather than co-operative learning alone, is considered to be most productive.

In addition, co-operative learning means more than merely assigning children to small groups. Teachers must also carefully design and prepare for the small-group setting. Students need instruction in skills necessary to operate successfully in small groups. Decisions must be made about the use of individual or group accountability. Care must be taken in establishing the mix of strengths and needs represented by students in the groups. Attention to these details will increase the likelihood that the co-operative groups will produce increased learning.

ADAPTIVE INSTRUCTION

Adaptive instruction is an integrated diagnostic-prescriptive process that combines several of the preceding practices-tutoring, mastery and co-operative learning, and instruction in learning strategies-into a classroom management system to tailor instruction to individual and small-group needs. The achievement effects of adaptive programmes have been demonstrated. The broader effects of adaptive instruction are probably underestimated, since it aims at diverse ends that are difficult to measure, including student autonomy, intrinsic motivation, teacher and student choice and parental involvement.

Adaptive education requires implementation steps executed by a master teacher, including planning, time allocation, task delegation to aides and students, and quality control. Unlike most other practices, it is a comprehensive programme for the whole school day, rather than a single method that requires simple integration into one subject or into a single teacher's repertoire. Its focus on the individual student requires that barriers to learning are first diagnosed and then a plan developed to address those needs. A student with special needs or experiencing academic difficulties becomes the shared responsibility of a team of teachers and specialists.

Such an approach to education calls for teachers to develop a broad spectrum of teaching approaches, along with knowledge of when to use each of them most productively, and to co-ordinate their efforts with those of other professionals providing support to a student.

Time and opportunity to do this are crucial for implementation of adaptive education. Skilful professional management is required to integrate all aspects of the programme. For example, curricular co-ordina-tion means more than a plan for the teaching of subject-matter skills and knowledge across grade levels as it applies to all students.

Instead, it encompasses the relationship of that curriculum to the abilities and needs of each student. Consequently, central-office staff, principals and teachers need more than usual training to install and maintain adaptive programmes. As goals for school become more clear and uniform, it should be increasingly possible to develop and employ systemic approaches, such as adaptive education.

BIBLIOGRAPHY

Chomsky, Noam, (1968), *Language and mind*, New York: Harcourt Brace Jovanovich.

Erikson, Erik, (1968), *Identity: Youth and crisis*, New York: Norton.

Gray, Peter, (1994), *Psychology*, New York: Worth.

Maccoby, Eleanor, (1974), *The psychology of sex differences*, Stanford, CA: Stanford University Press.

McShane, John, (1991), *Cognitive development: An information-processing approach*, Cambridge, MA: Basil Blackwell.

Piaget, Jean, (1929), *The child's conception of the world*, London: Routledge & Kegan Paul.

Vygotskii, L. S, (1997), *Educational psychology*, Trans. Robert Silverman. Boca Raton, FL: St. Lucie Press.

Eggen, P., & Kauchak, D., "The teaching of educational psychology: A research agenda", *Paper presented at annual meeting of the American Educational Research Association*, San Francisco.

Huitt, W. (Compiler), (1992), *Philosophy and education*, Valdosta, GA: Valdosta State University.

Sherman, L., (1995), "A post modern, constructivist pedagogy for teaching Educational Psychology, assisted by computer mediated communications", *Paper presentation to the CSCL95 Conference*, Bloomington Indiana.

Cerbin, W., (1999), "Advancing the scholarship of teaching: Pursuing the scholarship of teaching in educational psychology", *Paper presented at the 1999 Annual Meeting of the American Educational Research Association,* Montreal, Quebec.

Cerbin, W., (1992), *A learning centered course portfolio for educational psychology,* Unpublished manuscript.

Kuhn, D., (1999), *A developmental model of critical thinking,* Educational Researcher.

Marshall, H., (1998), *Teaching educational psychology: Learner-centered constructivist perspectives.* In N.M. Lambert & B.L. McCombs (Eds.) How students learn: Reforming schools through learner-centered education, Washington, DC: American Psychological Association.

INDEX

Other Books on

Education

1.	Modern Education for New Generation **(New)**	175/-
2.	Advanced Educational Technology **(New)**	175/-
3.	Comparative Education **(New)**	175/-
4.	Introduction to Educational Research **(New)**	175/-
5.	Computer Education **(New)**	175/-
6.	Teaching of Chemistry **(New)**	175/-
7.	Teaching of Physics **(New)**	175/-
8.	Handbook of Journalism & Mass Media **(New)**	225/-
9.	Advanced Educational Psychology **(New)**	175/-
10.	Educational Administration & Origanisation Management **(New)**	175/-
11.	Social Psychology **(New)**	225/-
12.	Teaching of Commerce **(New)**	175/-
13.	Educational Development & Technology **(New)**	175/-
14.	Disaster Management **(New)**	175/-
15.	Information Technology **(New)**	175/-
16.	Human Resource Development **(New)**	175/-
17.	Mass Media Communication **(New)**	225/-
18.	Adult Education **(New)**	175/-
19.	General Psychology **(New)**	175/-
20.	Distance Education in India **(New)**	175/-
21.	Teachers Education **(New)**	175/-
22.	Educational Philosophy **(New)**	175/-
23.	Science Teaching in Schools **(New)**	175/-
24.	Indian Polity **(Revised New)**	295/-
25.	New Comparative Government **(Revised New)**	295/-
Advance Study in the History of Modern India (PB)		
26.	(Volume-1: 1707-1813)	225/-
27.	(Volume-2: 1813-1920)	325/-
28.	(Volume-3: 1920-1947)	175/-
29.	Handbook of Nutrition & Dietetics **(New)**	250/-
30.	Development of Education in India	175/-

31.	A Text Book of Environmental Studies	175/-
32.	Teaching of History	175/-
33.	Administrative Thinkers	175/-
34.	Research Methodology	175/-
35.	Curriculum Development	195/-
36.	Teaching of Science	175/-
37.	Teaching of Mathematics	175/-
38.	Principles of Educational &Vocational Guidance	175/-
39.	Child Psychology	175/-
40.	Abnormal Psychology	175/-
41.	Indian Education in Emerging Society	175/-
42.	Human Resource Management	160/-
43.	Higher Education and Global Challenges	175/-
44.	Teaching of Geography	150/-
45.	Teaching of Social Studies	150/-
46.	Teaching of English	175/-
47.	Principles of Office Management **(Revised Ed.)**	250/-
48.	Education for All: The Indian Saga	175/-
49.	Value Education in Global Perspective	175/-
50.	Teacher Training	150/-
51.	Public Administration	150/-
52.	Public Relations & Integrated Communications	195/-
53.	Educational Psychology	175/-
54.	Introduction to Educational Technology	175/-
55.	Textbook of Food and Nutrition	150/-

INDEX

31.	A Text Book of Environmental Studies	175/-
32.	Teaching of History	175/-
33.	Administrative Thinkers	175/-
34.	Research Methodology	175/-
35.	Curriculum Development	195/-
36.	Teaching of Science	175/-
37.	Teaching of Mathematics	175/-
38.	Principles of Educational &Vocational Guidance	175/-
39.	Child Psychology	175/-
40.	Abnormal Psychology	175/-
41.	Indian Education in Emerging Society	175/-
42.	Human Resource Management	160/-
43.	Higher Education and Global Challenges	175/-
44.	Teaching of Geography	150/-
45.	Teaching of Social Studies	150/-
46.	Teaching of English	175/-
47.	Principles of Office Management **(Revised Ed.)**	250/-
48.	Education for All: The Indian Saga	175/-
49.	Value Education in Global Perspective	175/-
50.	Teacher Training	150/-
51.	Public Administration	150/-
52.	Public Relations & Integrated Communications	195/-
53.	Educational Psychology	175/-
54.	Introduction to Educational Technology	175/-
55.	Textbook of Food and Nutrition	150/-

Lotus PRESS

Unit No. 220, 2nd Floor, 4735/22,
Prakash Deep Building,Ansari Road, Darya Ganj,
New Delhi- 110002, Ph.: 32903912, 23280047
• E-mail : lotus_press@sify.com. www.lotuspress.co.in